HOPE AGAINST HOPE

Hope against Hope

Christian Eschatology
at the Turn of the Millennium

RICHARD BAUCKHAM and TREVOR HART

William B. Eerdmans Publishing Company
Grand Rapids, Michigan / Cambridge U.K.

© 1999 Richard Bauckham and Trevor Hart

First published 1999 by Darton, Longman & Todd Ltd
1 Spencer Court, 140-142 Wandsworth High Street, London SW18 4JJ

This edition published 1999 in the U.S.A. by
Wm. B. Eerdmans Publishing Co.
255 Jefferson Ave. S.E., Grand Rapids, Michigan 49503 /
P.O. Box 163, Cambridge CB3 9PU U.K.

Printed in the United States of America

05 04 03 02 01 00 99   5 4 3 2 1

ISBN 0-8028-4391-3

To Jürgen Moltmann

CONTENTS

ooooooooo

PREFACE
ooooooooo

Good Christian theology must be deeply and extensively
informed by the Bible and the Christian tradition, and at
the same time creatively alert and related to its particular
context. This book could not have been written before the
end of the twentieth century. It belongs to a time in which
the secular eschatologies of the modern age, that remarkable period of hopeful striving for a utopian future, have
lost credibility and even turned against hope. At such a
time it is vital that the Christian hope be rediscovered in
its own integrity and distinctive character. Only so can it
prove once again and afresh the hope in God for the
whole of God's creation that can resist a cultural loss of
future in the present. With this end in view, we find it
necessary to set 'hope against hope' – hope in the transcendent possibilities of God the Creator who gives his creation
future, against hope in the merely immanent possibilities
of human history that now threaten the future as much as
they promise to create it. Ours is a time for that radical
faith in God which Paul calls 'hoping against hope'
(Romans 4:18).

What we attempt in this book has three main characteristics. First, we intend to re-source Christian hope from its
rich resources in the biblical promises of God and the
Christian tradition of appropriating them in many ways.
Secondly, we do this in relationship with a diagnosis of our
western cultural context at the turn of the millennium, a

juncture which both prompts people to consider the future
and exposes the extent to which the modern ideology of
progress has failed and declined, leaving nothing to take
its place. Thirdly, we aim to restore the category of imagination to its essential role in Christian eschatology, both by
exploring the nature of eschatological statements and
by reflecting on the major images of the eschatological
future that the Bible and the tradition offer us. Christian
hope, we suggest, is not imaginary, but it is irreducibly
imaginative.

Truly collaborative work in constructive theology is rare,
as is the kind of interdisciplinary engagement of biblical
studies and systematic theology which we have attempted
in this book. One of the pleasures of writing it has been
the discovery of the ease with which our thinking and even
our writing styles have converged. We have each influenced
the other's thought and each written material that proved
completely consistent with the other's, hardly ever needing
to resolve differences or bridge gaps between us. So far
from generating the *odium theologicum* that such collaboration risks, the process has strengthened an intellectually
fruitful *amicitia theologica*. We shall be disappointed if
source critics manage to identify our respective contributions to the book, and have, to the best of our ability,
withheld any clues that might help them. In writing the
book we have happily relinquished a little of the scholarly
individualism that impels most of us theologians to lay sole
and possessive claim to our individual work. As far as we
are concerned, the final form of this text is wholly and
fully owned by us both.

Our warm thanks are due to Stephen Sykes, who invited
us to write in this series and offered helpful comments on
our text. The beginnings of our active collaboration on the
book lie in a tour of California in November 1997, when
we gave a joint lecture, 'Imaginative Hope – The Logic of

Looking Forward to the Future', at Bethel Seminary, San Diego, at Fuller Theological Seminary, Pasadena, and at Azusa Pacific University. At Westmont College, Santa Barbara, one of us, speaking to the title 'Approaching the Millennium', gave a first airing to other material that has since gone into the making of the book. We have happy memories of that very full week in California, and are most grateful to all who made us so welcome at the institutions we visited, as well as to the Deas Fund of St Mary's College, which partly financed the trip. Another joint lecture in which we developed some of the ideas of the book was given in the 1998 series of Lincoln Lectures in Theology; we thank Canon Vernon White for the invitation and the pleasure of his hospitality. Our co-authored paper on 'The Shape of Time', given at the 1999 meeting of the Society for the Study of Theology in Edinburgh, was written immediately after we completed the book; it both reflected and extended our thinking in the book. Also contributory to the ideas of the book were the Drew Lectures which each of us gave, one of us in 1996, the other in 1998, at Spurgeon's College, London; our thanks go to those who invited and entertained us on those enjoyable occasions. A course on Theology and Imagination which one of us has taught both in St Andrews and at Regent College, Vancouver, provided an opportunity to explore and develop some of the ideas contained in the book; thanks are due to the students whose critical reception of materials has helped to shape the outcome. Members of the Thursday lunchtime theological discussion group in St Andrews also discussed some of our ideas with us. Mark Bredin has compiled the indices for us. Finally, the synergy of our thinking owes a good deal to the congenial context of St Mary's College and to the quality of the beer at the Whey Pat Tavern, St Andrews.

Our debt to Jürgen Moltmann, to whom we have

dedicated the book, is probably to be seen more in the deep structures than on the surface of our work. Among the many influences that have gone into this book, his may well be the broadest, though we cannot be sure how well he will recognize his influence in what we have made of it. Not long before we embarked on this book, we had studied his eschatology together, discussed it with him, and written extensively on it in a volume devoted to his recent masterwork on eschatology.[1] In writing our own book, we were a little surprised at just how new and different, by comparison with his, our own treatment of eschatology has turned out to be. Others perhaps will be more struck by our affinity with his work. But in any case we gratefully acknowledge that, not only must any serious treatment of Christian eschatology at this time be in part an implicit dialogue with Moltmann, but also in our own case our book would not exist but for what we have learned from him and in dialogue with his theology.

1
ᴏᴏᴏᴏᴏᴏᴏᴏᴏᴏ

The Decline of Secular Hope

There's this thing called progress. But it doesn't progress.
It doesn't go anywhere. Because as progress progresses the
world can slip away.

(Graham Swift)[1]

MILLENNIAL STOCKTAKING

The first readers of this book will be well aware of the
approach of a new millennium. The western media are
unlikely to leave anyone within their reach unaware of it.
But, even apart from media, commercial and political
hype, the date itself, the year 2000, can hardly fail to
exercise a certain magic on anyone used to reckoning
years in centuries AD (or CE).

The way in which this magic works is rather more subtle
than we might at first think. At first sight we might suppose
it no more than a trick the calendar plays on us. Much as
our microchips threaten technological chaos on 1st
January 2000, because we have negligently programmed
them to do so, so the way of reckoning time which we
ourselves have devised happens to throw up a mind-bog-
gling date which could easily have been otherwise.
Informed people are now well aware that, on any probable
dating of the birth of Jesus Christ, its two-thousandth anniversary has already occurred several years before the year

1

2000. Our calendar is based on a miscalculation. But in any case, reckoning time in centuries and millennia, self-evident though it seems to us, is little more than an arbitrary convention. The Bible, for example, never does so; nor did most people for most of history or most Christians for most of Christian history. Were we concerned to follow a biblical model of calculating the times and the seasons, we should be counting not centuries, but generations, in sequences of sevens, tens or twelves. Or, with some ancient Jewish chronographers, we might use the jubilee (49 or 50 years) as the God-given way of periodizing history, and the significant dates would turn out to be quite different ones. The current sense of nearly unprecedented epochal meaning in the year 2000 *is* a trick our own calendrical magic is playing on us.

Nevertheless, there is more to be said about it. Surprisingly (since AD dates purport to be a Christian way of reckoning time), it is not the religious background that is most important here. It is true that there was an old Jewish and Christian notion of the world week, which is still alive in some Christian fundamentalist circles. It is this which makes the end of the *second* millennium AD significant in a way that the end of no other millennium could be. This tradition took Psalm 90:4 to mean that what Scripture calls one of God's 'days' is really, in our time, a thousand years, and on this rather dubious exegetical basis maintained that each of the six days of creation in the Genesis creation account represents a thousand years of world history. So the world will last six thousand years, followed by a thousand-year (or, in some versions of the theory, eternal) sabbath. If the creation of the world is dated around 4000 BC then the end of world history – the transition to the world's sabbath – will occur around 2000 AD.

This theory is really the only reason within the Christian tradition for attaching any particular significance to the two-thousandth anniversary of the birth of Jesus. It is the only context in which reckoning time in millennia has played any part in the Christian tradition. But clearly the credibility of the theory of the world week depends, not so much on the date of the birth of Jesus, as on the dating of creation. No one who thinks the world more than six thousand years old can have a Christian reason for finding the year 2000 significant. The theory of the world week is really just one of those many chronological speculations by which Christians have all too often tried to calculate the date of the end of history. Its biblical basis is as dubious as those of the others.

The New Age movement has its own reasons, astrological and prophetic, for expecting a qualitative leap in human consciousness and history to attend the advent of the new millennium. But these are not the most influential reasons for the magic of the year 2000. For most people who feel to some degree touched by that magic, the relevant ideological background is quite different. It is the modern idea of historical progress, a characteristically secular notion, though it has also taken religious forms. If we have been used to thinking of history as a kind of incremental progress of human civilization through time – and this has been the dominant myth of the modern western world – then it seems natural to take the ends of centuries as occasions for looking backwards and forwards, taking stock of the point we have reached in humanity's temporal advance. That we know centuries to be no more than a convenient way of measuring time that modern western people have invented need not deprive them of their significance, since it is human progress that we are using them to measure. Arbitrary measures they may be, but useful nonetheless. And if centuries can acquire this significance, how much more millennia!

3

Already in 1892, a columnist for the *Spectator*, the well-known British periodical, wrote this:

> The fact that we are approaching the end of another century of our era, strongly affects the popular imagination. It is supposed that, in some undefined way, we must be better or worse merely because of this chronological fact. Were it the end, not of the nineteenth [century], but of the twentieth, we should be still more excited. Even now, the idea of that Annus Mirabilis, the Year of Grace 2000, begins to affect us. We feel that if we could live to witness its advent, we should witness an immense event. We should almost expect something to happen in the Cosmos, so that we might read the great date written on the skies.[2]

The author's tone is a little ironic, but the mood he reflects is the famous *fin de siècle* mood of 1890s Europe. If *fin de siècle* – the end of the nineteenth century – created such an outpouring of angst and excitement, what, he not unreasonably wonders, would *fin de millénaire* – the approach of the third millennium – be like?

The *fin de siècle* mood of the 1890s entailed a process of assessment of the progress of civilization, at the end of a century whose élite, at least, considered it indisputably the century of progress, when civilization had advanced more than in the rest of human history. The process involved reviewing the past century and looking forward – enthusiastically or fearfully – into the next. The mood was an unstable mixture of optimism and pessimism, the assessment a kind of weighing of progress and decadence in the balance.

On the one hand, Max Nordau lamented the feeling of imminent perdition which he detected among intellectuals 'vague qualms of the Dusk of Nations, in which all suns and all stars are gradually waning, and mankind with all its institutions and creations is perishing in the midst of a dying world'[3], while, on the other hand, Frederic Harrison expressed the more prevalent, upbeat anticipation of a twentieth century propelled by the accelerating momentum of the nineteenth into a qualitatively better era:

> We *are* on the threshold of a great time, even if our time itself is not great. In science, in religion, in social organization, we all know what things are in the air. . . . It is the age of great expectation and unwearied striving after better things.[4]

Enthusiasm was not uncritical: there were end-of-century failures which required to be surmounted in the better future. So, rather in the spirit of new year resolutions, some writers offered new century resolutions.

Alfred Russel Wallace assessed the past century in a book called *The Wonderful Century* published in 1898 (notice, incidentally, how unlikely it is that a book published in 1998 could describe the twentieth century in such a title). He catalogued the extraordinary technological advances of the century, but castigated his contemporaries for neglecting hypnotism and phrenology while taking up the harmful practice of vaccination.[5] More significantly (so it seems with hindsight), he deplored the militarism which harnessed technological advance to the development of ever deadlier machines of war.[6]

But the dogmatic optimism of the century was not easily crushed. Alexander Sutherland, writing a year later under the title 'The natural decline of warfare', argued that a trajectory of progress over recent centuries pointed to the elimination of warfare in the not too distant future. At the end of the century, he pointed out, it was already the case that absolute peace reigned among civilized nations, though not yet on the borders of the civilized world[7] (the Anglo-Boer war began that same year, 1899). This is the kind of thinking that lay in the background to the devastating effect which the First World War was to have on progressivist optimism just a few years into the new century on which so much expectation had so recently been focused.

The intense cultural self-assessment which occurred at the end of the nineteenth century was unique to the nineteenth.[8] It is not the case that centuries' ends had regularly provoked such reflection. The sense of entering a new period which accompanied the end of the seventeenth and eighteenth centuries was minor by comparison, and previously there had been no such phenomenon at all. The reasons are twofold.

The first concerns what we have called the magic of the calendar. Until the seventeenth century few people noticed the year-date Anno Domini. For much of European history people had normally reckoned by the years of a king or by some local era, not by a world-historical era. Few seventh-century people, for example, knew that they lived in the seventh century.[9] Even when dating by the Christian era became common in official usage, ordinary people did not think in such terms. They did not use AD dates in letters or conversation. Our sense of living in a particular period defined as the umpteenth century probably began only in the sixteenth century, while it was the growing use of calendars in the seventeenth century that spread the typically modern sense of situating one's time in a numerical sequence of dates and centuries marking the forward march of a single human history.

It is noteworthy that the gradual dominance of AD dates in the western consciousness of time and history broadly coincided, not with the christianization of western society, but with its modernization. Though defined by its Christian reference-point, thinking AD was appropriate, perhaps even necessary, to the modern myth of historical

6

progress. The constant movement into an unlimited future, represented by the dates of the AD era as the universal movement of human history, enabled that sense of the accelerating advance of civilization that dominated the nineteenth century. Thinking in centuries works its calendrical magic not by accident, but because it coincides with the dominant myth by which the modern age has lived. That near-obsessive assessment of the past and future course of history, unique, among ends of centuries, to the 1890s, was unique precisely because it occurred at the end of the great century of progress, at the apogee of the myth of inevitable and unlimited human improvement.

So, at the end not just of the following century, but of the whole millennium, it is because the passing of AD time still evokes the myth of progress that the approach of the year 2000 stirs our imagination and provokes a sense of the need for stock-taking. But the power of the myth of progress is now, for most of us, the haunting power of its ghost. The twentieth century has drained almost all the life out of it, but it has so dominated and permeated the culture of modernity we cannot easily leave it behind. It will still be the spectre at many a millennial feast because we do not yet know what to put in its place and fear there is nothing at all to put in its place.

Thus the *fin de millénaire* is not turning out to be a *fin de siècle* to the power of ten. Books which take the turn of the millennium as a cue for a back-and-forth-looking assessment of where we are and how we should be aiming to get where we wish have been appearing steadily,[10] but even the optimists are highly chastened, while secular pessimism focuses not merely on decadence, as in the 1890s, but on truly apocalyptic danger. *Shall We Make the Year 2000?* (the title of a book published in 1985)[11] captures this mood.

One of the most recent of these stock-taking books,

called *The Age of Anxiety* (1996), aims to encounter the 'millennial anxiety', the fear of the future which character- izes British society in the 1990s. The book's authors themselves offer varying degrees, none too extreme, of optimism and pessimism. They take the anxiety seriously, and none proposes a return to the ebullient optimism of the nineteenth-century myth, on which the editors comment: 'For perfectibility read corruptibility, for belief in progress read naiveté.'[12] But it is surely no accident that the scientist among the authors retains more than his co- authors do of the nineteenth-century's faith in progress, science-based as that was to a large extent. He ends by exhorting us, 'if the going gets *really* anxious', to try to believe that science reassures.[13] But he would probably not be surprised if most of his readers failed to believe this. Increasingly, in public opinion, scientists are no longer benevolent magicians, but sorcerers' apprentices letting loose forces they cannot control and whose effects they cannot predict.

The difference from the 1890s resembles a paradigm shift. Then it was a matter of drawing up a balance sheet of successes and failures of the century: credit for building the railways, debit for stockpiling armaments, and so on. The difference now is not just that many find our balance sheet to be more or less in overall debit. Nor is it just that we disagree about the evaluation of many changes (is the decline of the traditional family progress or regress?). The most disturbing thing is that progress itself has turned threatening. Increasingly we have had to recognize that many of the most apparently benign advances of tech- nology are having calamitous results. The exponential continuation of the line of nineteenth-century progress is putting the future of the planet itself in the balance. The dominant myth by which the whole modern age has lived – the idea of historical progress – has not only failed us

8

but turned against us. The more we recognize this, the more the *fin de millénaire* must be a time, not just of taking stock of the past century, but of taking stock of the whole modern age. With the *fin de millénaire*, the time has come to assess not progress, but the myth of progress itself. But have we anything else with which to face the future?

The modern secular myth of progress was a 'metanarrative', one of those grand stories by which human societies and their individual members live. It was a kind of narrative sketch of the meaning of the whole of reality, subsuming this into human history pictured as a long march through time towards a utopian goal. Does the demise of this dominant myth of modernity mean we must now live without any such metanarrative, as many postmodernists propose? Can we manage with mere disillusioned pragmatism or hedonism? Can we live in the present without meaningful hope for the future? Are we content to celebrate the millennium as a postmodern game, enjoying the party as though there were no tomorrow?

Christian eschatology has an unavoidable stake in these questions. It is itself a metanarrative – or, rather, it is an indispensable part of the Christian metanarrative, the story which Christians tell about the meaning of the world, the narrative that runs from creation to consummation. Moreover, it resembles the modern myth of progress at least to the extent that it is orientated to the future and proffers ultimate hope for the future of the world. Indeed, the Enlightenment's idea of progress was certainly to some degree indebted to the Christian eschatology it repudiated. It has often been seen as a secularized form of the Christian metanarrative. So it is hardly surprising that in the modern period Christian eschatology has been in constant, changing relationships to the modern myth of progress. A responsible Christian eschatology for the new millennium must take full account of the decline of this myth.

THE DECLINE OF PROGRESS

The following account of the idea of progress is necessarily a simplification, since the idea has proved protean during the last two hundred years. But its broad outlines are clear. It originates in the European Enlightenment of the late eighteenth century (with older roots in the Renaissance). It expresses the Enlightenment's vast confidence that human reason, once freed from the shackles of traditional authority, prejudice and superstition, will take humanity into a new age of freedom and prosperity.

Much of the success of the idea of progress in the nineteenth century was connected with science and technology. A major key to human advancement was mastery of nature, coercing nature to serve human ends, reconstructing nature into a world more accommodating to human habitation, tapping the resources of nature for the material benefit of humans. A major factor powering this whole project of domination and advancement was economic. The relatively new idea that human wants and desires for material goods of all kinds were potentially unlimited made continuous economic growth a major imperative of western civilization. The typically modern economic process of creating constantly expanding demands in order to meet them was under way. The European colonial domination of large parts of the rest of the world in part served this economic aim which, as a matter of economic principle, pressed inexorably and insatiably into the indefinite future.

But progress was by no means conceived in purely material terms. Democratic freedoms and human rights evolved slowly but steadily from the principles of the

Enlightenment. The confidence in reason gave education a central role in progress, and, since human nature was understood as fundamentally rational and good, the dispelling of ignorance and the triumph of reason were confidently expected to lead to the general moral betterment of the race. Progress meant the steady progress of humanity towards perfection. Though highly Eurocentric, the myth of progress was universalistic in its goal. The rest of the world might require a long period of paternalistic rule by the West, but the extension of the benefits of European civilization to all was the ultimate goal of empire, at least according to the prevalent myth.

The idea of progress was common both to liberal progressivism and to Marxism, with the major difference that the former envisaged steady evolutionary change through the prolongation of the line of the present into the future, whereas the latter thought that progress could occur only through a dialectical process of class-conflict and revolution. The twentieth-century conflict between the liberal West and the communist East was a struggle for domination of the world by rather degenerate forms of the two major inheritors of Enlightenment progressivism.

One way of understanding and evaluating a metanarrative such as the myth of progress is to see it as a way of dealing with the horror of history and the terror of history. By the 'horror' of history, we mean all of the vast pain, suffering and loss which occur in human history, with the obstacle these pose for all attempts to find meaning in history. By the 'terror' of history,[14] we mean fear of the unpredictable and uncontrollable future, which always threatens attempts to maintain our happiness or to improve our lot. The idea of progress was designed to exorcize both.

More than any other ideology or worldview the myth of historical progress sought meaning within the process

11

of human history. Whereas Jewish and Christian views of history have looked to the transcendent God's activity within history and his intention and power to bring history to a meaningful conclusion, the Enlightenment typically abandoned transcendence in favour of wholly immanent meaning. The historical process itself contains and achieves its meaning. Belief in the inevitability of progress was thus a kind of faith in the process of history itself (replacing the Christian view of providence) to which human rationality found itself akin. Progress was the way the world was going, a belief strongly bolstered by the myth of biological evolution. (We call this too a 'myth' because we are not referring to evolution simply as a descriptive and scientifically explanatory account of biological change, but to the evaluation of this as an ever-ascending movement culminating and continued in human history.) Enlightened people were part of the process of the world's inherent tendency towards the goal of human perfection and domination of the world.

What then of the horror of history? It was the barbarism now steadily receding into the past. It was the eggs broken to make the utopian omelette. The idea of progress was a kind of immanent theodicy or *justification* of history. All the pains and losses were justified by the goal, whether this was conceived as a distant but finally to be achieved utopia or simply as never-ending progress. (Some theological interpretations of Darwinian evolution spoke of a 'law of sacrifice' as the engine of progress.) So long as the horror could be located predominantly in the past or beyond the bounds of European civilization, this theodicy seemed plausible to many. Everything negative in history was steadily being overcome. It is surprising how often even the idea that death will eventually be overcome surfaces in the utopian dreams of progress, even down to the present day (there are those who pay a great deal to have

12

their corpses preserved in the sure and certain hope of scientific resurrection one day). Liberal (as distinct from Marxist) progressivists can be virtually identified by their optimistic tendency to minimize the evils of the present. But the whole approach entails giving a radical evaluative priority to the future. It is not those who suffered the evils of the past – or even those suffering and dying in the present – who will benefit from progress, but those who increasingly come to profit at their expense.[15]

As we have already noticed, the presentation of the passing of time by means of centuries has a peculiar aptness to the idea of progress. It represents time in purely quantitative terms, and suggests the image of a line along which history moves into the future. It allows one to focus on the continuous, forward-moving advance, ignoring the discontinuities and the tragic losses of real history. The point becomes clear if we compare it with the model of time as the succession of generations, which was common in many traditional societies, including the biblical ones. Counting generations highlights the discontinuity of the generations passing away in death, as well as the continuity of the generations engendered and succeeding. Purely quantitative time, the homogeneous time that moves like a straight line into the future, ignores the tragedy and loss inherent in the historical process. It is as insensitive to human values as the relentless ticking of the clock that measures it.

It is no accident that such purely quantitative clock-time has come to dominate thinking about time in the era of the idea of progress. It is one way in which the latter attempts to tame the horror of history. But what of the terror of history? Here too the image of time as a forward-moving line is instructive. It encourages one to think of a single, set direction, in which the future continues a line running from the past through the present. It does not represent the unlimited openness of the future, from which any of an indefinite range of different possibilities – unpredictable, uncontrollable and often threatening – can occur in the present.

The idea of progress combines some sense of an immanent tendency towards utopia, inherent in the historical process, and a sense of human power through reason and technology to control the future. Sometimes, as in Marxism, historical inevitability and the exercise of human freedom to bring about the future goal seem to coexist in necessary, even if not fully consistent, complementarity. One is a kind of secularized version of the traditional Christian understanding of providence, the other a kind of human assumption of the responsibility for creating the future which had previously been in God's hands. Transcendence, in other words, is replaced both by immanent teleology and by human rationality and freedom. Together these surmount the terror of the future which had previously been avoided by trust in God.

Thus the power and responsibility for creating the future are seen as wholly human, but reassurance that human efforts to plan and to achieve the future are headed in the right direction come from the sense of a teleology inherent in the world system. Where the latter sense decays, as it has done in the twentieth century, confidence in progress comes to hang much more precariously on the ability of human power to shape the future according to rational planning. The terror of history must be mastered and dispelled by human control of the future. We encounter here again the characteristic notion of mastery that pervades the modern myth of progress. Human beings have mastered the course of history and are now controlling its future direction. Of course, this is very closely connected with technology, developed as the means of subjecting nature to human purposes.

14

The declining credibility – leading to virtual refutation – of the myth of progress in the twentieth century results from its inability to cope either with the horror of twentieth-century history or with the terror of the later twentieth century. The charge can be put even more strongly: the civilization that has made the idea of historical progress the myth by which it lives has itself increased both the horror and the terror of history.

We begin with the horror, which must surely be, to all whose vision is not ideologically distorted, one of the most prominent features of twentieth-century history. As George Steiner puts it, 'the period since August 1914 has been . . . the most bestial in recorded history.'[16] In wars and genocide, political torture and state terrorism – for which the two World Wars, the Holocaust, Stalin's reign of terror, Vietnam, and the killing-fields of Cambodia, Bosnia and Rwanda, can stand merely as representative instances, better remembered than many other horrors – literally hundreds of millions have died. This, of course, says far too little, for it fails to record the extremes of barbarity and the refinements of torment which easily equal those of any previous century. We must add the millions whose deaths from starvation were preventable but not prevented; those, including many children, still subjected to slave-labour no more tolerable than that of antiquity; and the (currently twenty-two) millions whom famine, war and oppression have made refugees or displaced persons.

In the face of such facts talk of moral progress becomes a sick joke. It might be more accurate to speak of moral regress. Perhaps it is not that human intentions have been more wicked, only that the technological means of effecting evil have increased. Or perhaps there are moral advances in other respects which must be weighed against the evils to which we have referred. But such moral arithmetic is not only impossible. It is also an inappropriately detached response to the incalculable horror of twentieth-century evil for anyone who attempts to contemplate it. No one with the moral sensitivity to feel its evil could bear it sufficiently to weigh it in any balance. Regress there may have been, progress there most certainly has not been.

The impact of twentieth-century evil on the idea of progress is even more devastating than we have yet appreciated. Not only do these horrors demonstrate the lack of progress. They also destroy any credibility the myth's 'theodicy' of history ever had. If these horrors are the price of progress, then progress is not progress. No utopian future can make these horrors acceptable or negligible or forgettable. How could any future progress compensate for children burned alive in Auschwitz or buried alive in Cambodia? (To borrow Ivan Karamazov's language, in Dostoevsky's classic discussion of theodicy, why must innocent children be the manure for other people's future happiness? If such suffering were the price of our entry to utopia, would we not, like Ivan, respectfully hand back the entrance ticket?[17]) Facing these horrors, we must surely conclude that history cannot be justified unless it can be justified to the dead. History can have no immanent meaning, unless it be a devilish one.

Furthermore, we must observe that both technology, on which the idea of progress sets so much hope, and the idea of progress itself are implicated in the horror. Technology in this century has abundantly proved its value for evil as well as for good. Its advances have made possible unprecedented destruction in war and more efficient state terrorism. Though nuclear weapons have been used only twice, it needs an unusually determined optimist to rule out their catastrophic use some time in the future. Futurologists are already predicting the imminent development of newly sophisticated biological weapons which will once again transform the character of war. As for the idea of

16

progress, not a few of this century's horrors have been committed precisely in the name of progress. Not only Nazi and Stalinist, but even liberal progressivist ideologies must share this blame. Breaking eggs to make the utopian omelette has become a regular practice in ideologically justified political atrocities. It becomes clear that the justification of history by progress is not only incredible, but also dangerous. If the horrors of the past can be accepted for the sake of future progress, then the horrors of the present can be perpetrated for the sake of progress.

In the last paragraph we have already hinted at the way the myth of progress has failed to dispel the terror of the future in the second half, at least, of the twentieth century. What has happened is that the great modern project to master nature and the future through technology has paradoxically itself become a threat. Many hitherto unforeseen effects of 'progress' are conspiring to achieve already widespread ecological destruction and to threaten the very future of the planet. But, even to the extent that ways of avoiding the worst effects are now known, it seems impossible to control the technological and economic juggernaut which seems now to be hurtling without a driver towards Armageddon. It appears driverless because the real drivers are those of us who make up the affluent élite of the world, those who continue to pursue economic growth while consuming the world's resources and destroying its ecosystems at a rate with which others could not catch up without catastrophe for the planet. We are in the driver's seat, but the ghost of progress sits at our side.

The point is not that catastrophe is actually inevitable, but that it can easily seem so, because the route to it is the continuation of the route we used to consider the sure route to utopia. Even apart from the considerable pain of kicking our addiction to material consumption and novelty, we are in a dilemma. The future seems out of control, but it is precisely the attempt to control the future which has created the present threat. Should we simply intensify our faith in the technological project, trusting it to get us out of the hole it has put us in, or should we relapse into helpless fatalism? Are there any other options?

We must hammer one more nail into the coffin of the idea of progress. In our now 'postmodern' age, as many regard it, the modern metanarrative of progress has been a main target of critique from those – 'postmodernists' – who wish most self-consciously to put modernity behind them and to expose its illusions. (It is useful to distinguish between 'postmodernity' – or, as some prefer, 'late modernity' – which is the period in which Enlightenment culture is rapidly declining, and 'postmodernism', which is an intellectual and cultural movement contending for the succession to Enlightenment culture.) From a postmodernist perspective the myth of progress looks like an ideology of domination. It has legitimated the exploitative exercise of power: the domination of the West over the Third World, the affluent over the poor, even men over women. Through science, technology and education the West has imposed its own particular rationality and ideals on others, claiming the particular values of a western élite to be universal, overriding and replacing indigenous cultural traditions. While this critique may well be exaggerated, it is easy to recognize truth in it.

We may add that, as well as universalizing its own perspective, the West's promotion of 'progress' has signally failed to implement the principle of human equality which belongs to the originating ideals of the myth of progress. Technological development and economic growth have increased rather than decreased inequality, both within the affluent countries of the West, and in the economic relationships of the West with the rest of the world, as also

18

between the westernized élites of 'developing' countries
and the mass of their population.

Moreover, of the changes which seem most unequivo-
cally beneficial to human life, it is hard to think of many
which have yet benefited the poor majority of the world's
population. We can no longer be comforted by the illusion
that what the West already has will inevitably in time also
benefit the 'developing' world. This is partly because the
dynamic of the process does not seem in fact to be taking
this course, but also because the process is everywhere
coming up against ecological limits. While the Americaniz-
ation of global culture has made the American standard
of living the standard to which all aspire, the American
standard of living itself makes it objectively impossible for
most of the world to share it.

Why does the ghost of the idea of progress still stalk the
corridors of power and the homes of affluent people like
most readers of this book? It is partly because there are
two spheres in which it still has much influence. One is
the scientific community, where the scientistic myth of
unambiguous progress through scientific and technological domination of nature is still the ideological context
in which many practising scientists think. The desultory
and far too rare discussions of a whole range of developments in bio-engineering in recent years have shown how
far scientists pursuing their own research cannot compre-
hend the well-founded doubts and fears of many of the
public.

The other field in which the idea of progress dies hard
is that of professional politicians, whose perceived freedom
of action and imagination tends to be so circumscribed as
to strongly favour the continuation of the direction in
which the line from the past through the present points.
But for most of us there is also another factor. In one
sense, the demise of the idea of progress does not put our

society in a novel situation, since most societies – both in Europe before the eighteenth century and elsewhere also down to this century – have lived without any idea of progress. But we differ in that we have still to live with the exponentially increasing rate of change which the modern project of technological domination powered and which still continues. The idea of progress enabled people to welcome rapid and radical change. Though there were once Luddites, the term increasingly became derogatory as the culture of progress gained popular currency. But without the confidence that change must be progress, change has become disorientating and threatening. Having to evaluate specific changes is very demanding, while trying to affect the direction of change can be depressingly ineffective. Easily enough the image of progress transmutes into its opposite: the driverless juggernaut heading for Armageddon.

Finally, we should be clear that this little funeral oration for the idea of progress is not a way of rubbishing all the real achievements of the modern period. What is at issue is the 'metanarrative' by which the modern age has very self-consciously understood itself. It is this that has shaped the nature and direction of change and brought us to our present very critical juncture of history. We find ourselves caught in the contradictions of modernity, and have not yet found a way forward.

ANTI-METANARRATIVES

Before turning in the next chapter to the Christian metan-arrative, we shall consider three anti-metanarratives, as one might call them, all three formulated in deliberate oppo-sition to the modern myth of progress. In their different ways all three throw considerable light on the decline of the myth of progress and the condition of western society after its end. Their authors are all seminal thinkers. We consider them here in chronological order.

First, the German philosopher Friedrich Nietzsche (1844–1900), a postmodern thinker in the heyday of modernity, pioneer of much that we now think characteristically postmodernist.[18] Famously, Nietzsche proclaimed the death of God, i.e. the loss of credibility of the idea of God in the modern period. He proclaimed it as an event whose unprecedented significance had not yet been perceived even by the atheists of Nietzsche's time. The death of God entails the end of truth and morality as objective and universal values. For the typically modern, humanist atheism which found inherent meaning in the historical process as progress towards a goal Nietzsche had only scorn. It was merely an atheistic continuation of Christian values. It had failed to see that the death of God entailed also the death of meaning and progress in history. Nietzsche in effect foresaw the incredulity towards all metanarratives which a century later would be said to define the postmodern (see below). The death not only of the Christian metanarrative but also of its stepchild the modern myth of progress follow from the death of God.

In their place Nietzsche offered an anti-metanarrative: the idea of eternal recurrence. Postmodernists have in this respect not followed Nietzsche, but the idea plays an important role in his thought. We can think of it as the antithesis of any metanarrative that seeks meaning in history or in eschatology. Nietzsche presents it vividly like this:

> What, if some day or night a demon were to steal after you into your loneliest loneliness and say to you: 'This life as you now live it and have lived it, you will have to live once more and innumerable times more; and there will be nothing new in it, but every pain and every joy and every

21

thought and sigh and everything ultimately small or great in your life will have to return to you, all the same succession and sequence – even this spider and this moonlight between the trees, and even this moment and I myself. The eternal hourglass of existence is turned upside down again and again, and you with it, speck of dust!'

Would you not throw yourself down and gnash your teeth and curse the demon who spoke thus? Or have you once experienced a tremendous moment when you would have answered him: 'You are a god and never have I heard anything more divine.' If this thought gained possession of you, it would change you as you are or perhaps crush you. The question in each and every thing, 'Do you desire this once more and innumerable times more?' would lie upon your actions as the greatest weight. Or how well disposed would you have to become to yourself and to life *to crave nothing more fervently* than this ultimate eternal confirmation and seal?[19]

The idea of eternal recurrence functions as a kind of illumination of what it would really mean to accept fully the lack of meaning and purpose in the world. To live without a metanarrative, liberated from the Christian and modern dream of a reality different from what actually is, should mean to be able instead to affirm the totality of life just as it is, to crave nothing more fervently than that one's actual life, just exactly as it has been and is, should recur infinitely. But Nietzsche himself knew that it would take the Superman to be able to do that. It must mean, for example, that survivors of Auschwitz must crave nothing more fervently than that the sufferings of Auschwitz recur, just as they happened, infinitely.

Auschwitz, as we have seen, is a good test of both meta-narratives and anti-metanarratives. As representative of the evils of the twentieth century, Auschwitz negates the myth of progress. The modern attempt to find meaning inherent in history founders on Auschwitz, but does not Nietzsche's rejection of meaning also? Who would not say that to affirm Auschwitz as part of the totality of life, to want nothing to be different, to crave its eternal recurrence, would be not super- but subhuman?

Nietzsche died long before Auschwitz. Walter Benjamin, the German Jewish philosopher, died a year before Hitler decreed the Final Solution. But Benjamin already saw the reality of his time as one of mass murder when he wrote, only months before his own death in 1940, the following meditation on a painting by Paul Klee which he owned and which had long fascinated him:

> A Klee painting named 'Angelus Novus' [the new angel] shows an angel looking as though he is about to move away from something he is fixedly contemplating. His eyes are staring, his mouth is open, his wings are spread. This is how one pictures the angel of history. His face is turned toward the past. Where we perceive a chain of events, he sees one single catastrophe which keeps piling wreckage upon wreckage and hurls it in front of his feet. The angel would like to stay, awaken the dead, and make whole what has been smashed. But a storm is blowing from Paradise; it has got caught in his wings with such violence that the angel can no longer close them. This storm irresistibly propels him into the future to which his back is turned, while the pile of debris before him grows skyward. This storm is what we call progress.[20]

The typically modern view of history as inevitable progress looks resolutely forward, but Benjamin through the staring eyes of his angel of history faces backwards, his eyes fixed on the victims and the wreckage of history that pile up before him. Progress leaves the victims behind. The future cannot repair the past. What Benjamin sees so clearly is that history cries out for redemption and progress cannot provide it. Even were the angel to be finally blown to a standstill in utopia, the debris of history would remain before his eyes. Utopia can be no compensation for those who have suffered history. It leaves the dead dead. While Benjamin, in this bleakly back-to-front vision of progress, offers no hope for the redemption of history, he refutes any notion that the modern metanarrative can offer such hope.

The French philosopher who famously in 1979 defined the postmodern as 'incredulity towards metanarratives',[21] Jean-François Lyotard, offers an anti-metanarrative of his own, which he calls a postmodern fable.[22] It tells in purely scientific terms the story of the origin of the earth, the process of Darwinian evolution, and the story of humanity up to the time, many millions of years in the future, when the sun is about to explode and absorb the solar system into itself. Whatever it is that the human brain has then become escapes the catastrophe by leaving the planet forever before its destruction. This can be thought possible because the human species will have foreseen and pre-pared for the death of the solar system millions of years before it happens.

Nevertheless the story has no human meaning. It is not the story of human beings, but of energy. It is the story of the conflict between the two processes that affect energy: entropy and increasing differentiation or complex-ification. The former leads to the death of the solar system, but the latter makes possible the escape of the highly complex form of organizing energies into which the human species will have evolved by then. That will not be humanity but as different from us as the human species is from the amoeba. Humans are merely one transitory form in which energy is organized. The escape, with which the fable ends, cannot be an object of human hope as utopia

24

has been for modern progressive humanity, for it is not humans who escape, and, in any case, the hero of the fable is not humanity or even what humanity will then have become, but energy. Humans are objects of history, not subjects, and even energy is not the subject of history, for it has no intentionality.

The fable is postmodern in that its content signifies 'the end of hopes (modernity's hell)', as Lyotard puts it,[23] while the form is no more than a fable, self-consciously imaginary. It expresses what Lyotard calls 'the postmodern state of thought': the 'suffering for lack of finality', which eschatology, Christian and modern, used to assuage, but the postmodern fable cannot. The fable seems appropriate to our situation at the turn of the millennium, when there seems considerable interest in scientific cosmology and Darwinian evolution. As substitutes for the grand narratives of religion and modernity, these scientific narratives can only be anti-metanarratives, offering explanation but not meaning.[24] It remains to ask whether the Christian meta-narrative, with its orientation to the eschatological future, can provide the genuine hope which the myth of progress has in the end failed to provide and to which the anti-progressivist anti-metanarratives do not aspire.

2

oooooooooo

The Hope of an Ending

If only there were endings. If only the moment arrived when
there was no more longing, and the story froze and was
stilled beyond grief and disappointment and age and death.
(Niall Williams)[1]

END OF STORY?

It is arguable that, whereas pre-modern (traditional)
societies gave priority to the past and modern (progressive)
society gave priority to the future, with the decline of the
idea of progress a postmodern society is emerging in which
priority is given to the present. In contemporary western
society, with its throwaway culture, its emphasis on the
immediate and the instantaneous, its feverish drive to
squeeze as much as possible into time as a limited com-
modity, its fragmentation of time into allocated quantities,
and its obsessive organization of time, we live increasingly
in the present and its prolongation. More than one
observer speaks of the 'compressed time' in which we live.[2]

More and more rapid change and the pressure to focus
on the present as a duration to be used and filled with
activity cut us off from continuity with the past. History is
not part of a story we ourselves are living, merely a theme-
park we visit for amusement. The future, on the other
hand, is shrinking to a short-term prolongation of the

26

present, that future which we can extrapolate from the present, the future we have already allocated and planned, the future of long-range diaries, government think-tanks, millennium projects. It is the future already contained in the present, not the sphere of the unpredictable and the unexpected, of an indefinite range of possibilities which might eventuate.

Thus Helga Nowotny, who speaks of 'what nostalgically is still called the future', predicts 'the abolition of the category of the future and its replacement by the idea of an extended, but manageable and controllable, present'.[3] Though she denies that choice and surprise will be thereby eliminated, they are clearly to be contained within a firm framework of control. It is paradoxical that this virtual elimination of the future is the long-term result of the success of modernity's great technological project to master the future. Whereas nineteenth-century utopianism combined the dream of mastery with the magic of the future as the sphere of vast hopes, the apparent achievement of mastery has closed off the future.

But there is a more sinister aspect to the idea that the future is becoming controllable. Insofar as humans determine the future, it comes about as the result of the interaction of innumerable choices and decisions made by many people. This is in part what makes it unpredictable, in that people are unpredictable and the results of the conjunction of their choices even more so. Control of the future is conceivable only if people's choices are also managed and controlled. A world truly without future will be a world in which everything, including people, will be completely managed by bureaucratic administration.

This is precisely the dream – or nightmare – of a 'post-historical' age which not a few thinkers have entertained since the nineteenth century. It will be post-historical in the sense that there will no longer be freedom or contingency, no unpredictable novelty, and thus no 'history'.[4] It is not only Christian eschatology that speaks of the end of history: Hegel, Marx, Comte, and most recently Francis Fukuyama[5] have done so too. History ends when there are no longer any alternatives. This is the result to which the pursuit of progress, understood as rational and techno-logical mastery of the future, logically leads. The modern 'metanarrative' is reaching its conclusion, and the emerging postmodern or 'post-historical' age lives 'happily ever after' in a present without future.

Fukuyama's is a rather mild (as well as peculiarly blinkered)[6] version of this idea. He argues that with the collapse of communism, there is now no alternative to liberal democracy and the free market economy. In effect, one version of the idea of progress (liberal progressivism) has won its conflict with the other version (Marxism) and proved the one which will consummate the modern meta-narrative in the end of history. But the progressivist metanarrative seems to exemplify the contention that it is better to travel than to arrive: 'The end of history will be a very sad time' (Fukuyama).[7]

However, the idea that progress is reaching its fulfilment in a post-modern present without future must be seriously questioned. It is an interpretation of the present in the light of the idea of progress, rather than in the light of the failure of the idea of progress which we observed in the last section. The project to control the future now threatens the world with apocalyptic catastrophe, which will certainly not be avoided by continuing further along the same road. A different future, not the mere pro-longation of the present, needs to be imagined and chosen. We need a new respect for the limits of planning, prediction and control, and a vision that transcends the short-termism of political and bureaucratic management.

Although it is true that we live more and more in the

'compressed time' of the crammed and organized present, we also live with 'the tension, so unbearable that the effort is made to bury it deep in the unconscious, between the pressures of the moment and the uncertain times that lie ahead'.[8] Psychologically, our immersion in the immediate and the manageable is also an avoidance of the terror of the open future which seems to threaten more than it invites hope. Insecurity of employment, increasing crime and disintegrating social order, environmental catastrophe, and other terrors lurk in the uncontrollable future of that majority of British people who tell the pollsters they think that things are getting worse. The greater the technological control, the greater the anxiety about its uncontrollable effects.[9]

Postmodernists also celebrate the present without past and future, now that history has ended. In their case, history has ended, not in the modernist sense that the modern metanarrative has reached its conclusion, but in the sense that there can be no more metanarratives. In the famous sentence already quoted in our previous chapter, Jean-François Lyotard defined the postmodern as 'incredulity towards metanarratives'.[10] This rejection of any kind of grand story about the whole of reality is rooted, on the one hand, in applying a hermeneutic of suspicion to the idea of progress, exposing it as an ideology of domination, as we noticed in the last chapter. All such metanarratives, by claiming universality for what can only be a particular perspective or tradition, suppress difference and oppress others. (At first sight it looks as though Christian eschatology must suffer this critique along with the secular eschatology of progress.) But this rejection of metanarratives, on the other hand, also entails the postmodernist epistemology in which texts are about texts and ideas about ideas, in a continual regress that allows no grasp on non-linguistic reality.

The following quotation from 'A Post-Modern Manifesto' puts it with rather crudely Nietzschian extremism:

> We must learn to live after truth. . . . We tell a tale of
> nihilism in two stages: relativism and reflexivity. When we
> consider the status of our theories and our truth, we are
> led to relativism. Relativism, in turn, turns back on itself
> and disappears into the vicious spiral of reflexivity. Nothing
> is certain, not even this. . . . This is no ordinary time. The
> modern age opened with the destruction of God and
> religion. It is ending with the threatened destruction of all
> coherent thought. The age was held on course by stories of
> progress and emancipation. . . . But these stories are now
> exhausted. There are no new stories to replace them. . . .
> The paradigm for constructing paradigms is now
> collapsing. . . . The only political ideals left are those of the
> cynical and the paranoid. Such disillusion has lurked in
> the wings of European culture for two centuries. Now it can
> command centre stage. We are paralyzed by the perform-
> ance and we cannot leave the theatre. All the exits are
> blocked.[11]

So far from offering a way out of the contradictions of
modernity, postmodernism appears to resolve them in a
dead end from which there is no escape.

Radical postmodernism is a challenge to the understanding of Christian faith as story which has become
popular in recent theology and to which we have already
appealed in claiming eschatology as integral to the
Christian metanarrative. The critique of metanarratives as
ideologies of domination we shall have to confront later.
But the postmodernist deconstruction of mimetic imagination extends to the deconstruction of all narratives,
whether historical, fictional or autobiographical. The unity
and coherence which stories give to past, present and
future, the personal identity which the narrative of one's

life gives one, are mystifying constructions which can be deconstructed. Postmodernist time fragments into disconnected presents. Postmodernism proclaims not merely the end of this or that grand story, but the end of story.

THE SENSE OF AN ENDING

However, it is doubtful whether we are really witnessing the end of narrativity. Even in the compressed present which most of us inhabit much of the time, human experience remains inescapably temporal. As Barbara Hardy puts it, narrative is not merely

> an aesthetic invention used by artists to control, manipulate and order experience, but a primary act of mind transferred to art from life itself. . . . For we dream in narrative, daydream in narrative, remember, anticipate, hope, despair, believe, doubt, plan, revise, criticise, construct, gossip, learn, hate and love by narrative.[12]

Our temporal experience has become more fragmented, less amenable to representation as a unidirectional story, but we can scarcely speak of it at all without narrative. In the totally organized 'post-historical' world there would be no new stories, only planned behaviour and predictable outcomes, but we have already found in that world no more than a mythical product of the idea of progress.

In postmodernism all stories become unpretentious and playful fictions, but for all the disruptions of linear narrative and subversions of narrative meaning to be found in postmodernist fiction, narrative is never entirely abandoned, and the effects are often dependent on readers' awareness of the conventions of narrative realism which they dismantle. Narrative is interrogated and deconstructed, but not replaced. In popular culture, story – whether in film, drama, novel, biography, or comic strip –

31

continues to flourish, while soap operas appear to be the most indispensable staple of all television schedules. The narrative tradition in all media constantly plays with deconstructive elements: they improve the game rather than bringing it to an end.

Frank Kermode, in his well-known book *The Sense of an Ending*, takes a moderately postmodern position. Narrative imposes form and order on the inherently chaotic world ('we are surrounded by [chaos], and equipped for co-existence with it only by our fictive powers'[13]). Narrative assuages the horror of history by humanizing the utterly inhuman: 'Fictions deceive us in order to console us.'[14] Essential to this function is the end to the story. Plots move through time to an end which confers meaning on the whole. This point is extremely important because it rightly focuses the question of the relationship of story to reality on the ending of a story. While plots, as Kermode argues, can incorporate contingency, though never sufficiently to be true to life, the ends of plots flatly contradict the always unconcluded nature of life. Thus it is in reaching an ending that most 'realistic' fictions seem at the same time least true to reality and most aesthetically satisfying.

There are in fact fictional stories without conclusions. Kermode, writing about novels, ignores the soap opera, a narrative genre which has only become possible with radio and television, since it depends on paralleling real time. The Archers eat their Sunday lunch at the same time as the rest of us. Soap operas therefore provide their addicts with an ongoing narrative temporally parallel to the stories of their own lives, seeking meaningful form but always lacking conclusion.

Other narratives have in some sense to end. There are novels which attempt open-endedness, the plot not fully resolved but open to further inconclusive developments, and films which, for commercial reasons, leave a chink open to possible sequels. But many narratives continue to satisfy our wish to see all loose ends tied up or closure contrived by some aesthetically appropriate gesture. Brian Wicker, developing Kermode's argument, considers it an advantage of such 'strong endings' that their obvious fictiveness helps 'to remind us that what we have been through is only a story'.[15] They help to prevent stories degenerating into myths, which are stories whose ends are taken to be real.

But if such endings only remind us that life is not really like that, will not our satisfaction in them be intolerably contradicted by this reminder? As Kermode says, it is 'so desolately' that we know 'that *as* [fiction] and *is* [real life] are not really one'[16] – and never will be.[17] Can we actually live with Kermode's bleakly postmodern conviction that the sense of an ending is a necessary fiction by which we make sense of a senseless world? If we really accept that *as* can never be *is*, can we go on colluding with the false consolation that fictional ends give us?

The novelist Gustave Flaubert said that, 'Real life is always misrepresented by those who wish to make it lead up to a conclusion. God alone may do that.'[18] The gulf which the sense of an ending creates between narrative *as* and real *is* can be understood nihilistically, but it can also be understood eschatologically: only God can supply a conclusion to real life, but God will do so. Our quest for narrative meaning in our own lives and our satisfaction with the achieved narrative meaning of the fictional happy ending are implicitly eschatological, seeking the narrative meaning which the end of history will achieve.

The point is made in a somewhat different way by Wolfhart Pannenberg, who argues that all apprehensions of meaning implicitly anticipate the end of history.[19] Since all reality is historical, the truth of things must be sought in what they turn out to be in the end. Since all reality is intrinsically interconnected, the meaning of any part is not finally separable from that of the whole. The meaning of an individual's life requires a wider social context of meaning which in turn requires a wider historical context of meaning. . . . Only when history is completed will the final meaning of all things – and hence of each thing – be achieved.

The sense of an ending which the quest for narrative meaning seems necessarily to entail suggests that either reality cannot satisfy this quest or it will do so eschatologically. In the latter case, we can say that narrative corresponds to reality without meaning in some naive way that it is a transcript of what actually happens. Narratives are always highly selective and strongly perspectival. (This is why the story of Jesus, the story which is decisive for the Christian metanarrative, comes to us not in one but in four different canonical versions.) The stories we tell about real life and history, to the extent that they respect contingency and contradiction while aspiring to plot and resolution, really touch on the meaning God is making out of the world. They need not be untrue, but they are necessarily provisional and never complete. In the satisfying conclusions we know to be fictional we express the hope for the truly satisfying conclusion in reality that can only come at the end of history.

There is a sense in which some kinds of pre-modern narratives manifest this in a way that contemporary readers and audiences, as a result of modernist realism, no longer appreciate. The 'happily ever after' ending, conventional in folk-tales, was always palpably 'unrealistic'. The ridicule it has standardly evoked in the modern period simply misses the point.[20] (The marriages at the end of Jane Austen's novels are a later version of this convention.) The way in which Shakespeare's often sprawlingly untidy plots can nevertheless conclude with a remarkably contrived knotting of every loose end sometimes has contemporary audiences quite inappropriately laughing. But laughter is one kind of postmodern response to the incongruity of *as* and *is*.

Wicker, as we have noticed, prefers the most 'unrealistic' endings because they highlight the fictional nature of narrative as such. There is another reason for us to prefer them. Since they do not eventuate from any realistically plausible plot, they do not suggest that the historical process itself will result in a meaningful end. They do not correspond to the immanent eschatology of the idea of progress. Perhaps it is no accident that the heyday of realism in imaginative literature was roughly contemporaneous with the heyday of the myth of progress. Now that we know that history will not of its own accord produce utopia, we are better placed to appreciate the *deus ex machina* type of ending. From an eschatological perspective, the more improbable the better! The more improbable, the truer! For the only credible eschatology, given the failure of the myth of progress, is a transcendent one, which looks for a resolution of history that exceeds any possible immanent outcome of history. Only from the transcendent possibilities of God can this world be given a satisfying conclusion.

THE STORY OF ALL STORIES

It is time to turn to the Christian metanarrative,[21] with its eschatological conclusion. Our task is to see how it offers a way beyond the contradictions of modernity, such as postmodernism fails to offer. The Christian metanarrative, of course, is the biblical story of the world from creation to consummation. It is the story of the trinitarian God's relationship with his creation. It sees God as the beginning and end of all things, their source and their goal,

Creator and Lord, Redeemer and Renewer, the one who was and who is and who is to come. It shares with the Jewish and Islamic metanarratives, but few others before modern times, the characteristic of a story which is not yet completed. It is not, for example, a cosmic myth, complete in its own primal time, into which people must enter in order to renew time from its mythic source. The end of the story is still to come, with the God who is also to come to his creation in the end.

This means that those who live by this story live within it. It gives us our identity, our place in the story, and a part to play in the still-to-be-completed purposes of God for his world. Indeed, the story is told precisely so that people may live by it. As a story of the whole world and God's relationship to the world it is no more than a patchy outline, narrated in vivid historical detail in parts, sketched in non-realistic form in others, and concluded, necessarily, only in imaginative pictures of what is yet to come. Large areas of the world and huge tracts of world history occur in it only by implication when it speaks of all peoples and the whole world. Such features, which would be unsatisfactory were the story to serve some other purpose, are no obstacle to the purpose it actually serves. It tells us all we need to live by, to live within the story, to live in continuity with the decisive events of its past and in expectation of its still future conclusion.

At the heart of the metanarrative is the decisive story, that of Jesus, in whom God is accomplishing his purpose of redeeming his creation from evil and renewing it in glory. The story of Jesus, like the whole story, is unconcluded and cannot be concluded apart from the conclusion of the whole story. In some eucharistic liturgies the acclamation is used: 'Christ has died; Christ is risen; Christ will come again.' In this declaration the whole world is encompassed in God's loving and redemptive purpose.

In Jesus' death God's love has identified with all humanity in their wickedness and evil, pain and death. In Jesus' resurrection the new creation has already happened representatively to one human being for the sake of all others. In Jesus' future coming, God is coming to his creation to take it beyond all evil and death into the glory of his own presence. The declaration also places us in the meantime, in which the Spirit of Jesus is active in the mission of the church to the world, with the news of God's love for all and the hope of God's coming to all. In this activity of the Spirit the new creation is already being anticipated in provisional forms in human life.

It is important to distinguish this metanarrative clearly from modernity's myth of progress, which succeeded it as the dominant myth of European culture. It is important to do this, because for two reasons the distinction has often been fudged. One reason is the historical attempt to understand the origin of the modern metanarrative as a development from the Christian metanarrative. There is truth in this, but as we shall see, the discontinuity is at least as important as the continuity, and it does not help historical understanding of the modern age to play down the real novelty of its metanarrative.

The other reason why the distinction has often been fudged is that Christian theologians have frequently tried to give theological legitimation to modernity by claiming its major characteristics to be based on Christian premises. In so doing they have assimilated the Christian metanarrative to liberal progressivism. That assimilation still lingers not only in the expected but in quite surprising Christian places. But it is worth noticing how badly this uncritical theological endorsement of modernity has backfired on Christianity. Postmodernists, greens and others who observe the failure of modernity and the damage its myth of progress is doing often blame Christianity as the ideological source of the modern age. Liberal theologians could be said to have asked for this anti-Christian misreading of history. At least they should serve as warning to contemporary theologians not to follow suit in an uncritical theological endorsement of postmodernism.

What essentially happened in the Enlightenment origins of the myth of progress was the loss of transcendence and the reduction of eschatology to the immanent goal of human history. The end of history and the new creation had not in the Christian tradition been considered the end-product of the historical process (and in that sense the goal of history), but a fresh creative act of the transcendent God who would thus make of his creation what it had no immanent capacity to be. Nor had the activity of the Spirit in anticipating the new creation within history normally been seen as a cumulative process bringing the world gradually into the perfection of the kingdom of God. Moreover, the coming kingdom of God was not understood as merely the final period of history, to be reached at the end of a continuous line stretching into the future. The end of history was to happen to the whole of history, entailing the resurrection and the judgement of all the dead. This is eschatological transcendence which necessarily disappeared with God when Enlightenment humanity replaced God by taking the reins of history into their own hands.

In doing so they took over far more of the Christian eschatological hope than mere history without transcendence could bear. Education and technology were now the means to the goal of history, which could only be understood as an immanent goal, the product of the historical process. By these means human beings were perfectible and the world infinitely adaptable to human needs. Education replaced grace and technology replaced creation. The whole scientific-technological project of the modern age has been a kind of new creation, a remaking of the world, as though humans had the creative power of God and the creative wisdom of God.

This was promethean eschatology which crucially failed to recognize the limits of this world. In assuming limitless power over a limitless future of unlimited resources, humanity reached for the eschatological freedom of God and is now discovering the limits only as we collide catastrophically against them. As a quite secular reflection puts it:

> We have paid too little attention to the fact that we are limited and mortal – one reason being perhaps that Nietzsche's dictum 'God is dead' suggests that we claim God's empty place for ourselves. What is called for now is that we take our intrinsic limitedness seriously and understand the limitations of reason and of our possibilities endlessly to manipulate the world. The interplay of what we are able to do and what is not dependent on us has to be newly determined and reflected on.[22]

So it is high time Christian theology broke its long habit of legitimating prometheanism by interpreting the modern age as nothing more than humanity's assumption of the God-given powers and responsibility of the creature made in God's image. This has been theological collusion in the modern rape of creation and the murder of all the victims of twentieth-century progress.

How then can Christian eschatology, thus distinguished from the myth of progress, deal with the horror of history and the terror of history as we face them at the end of the twentieth century? Unlike the myth of progress, Christian eschatology does not privilege future history over past history. The end of history will happen to all of history. In the resurrection all the dead of all history will rise to judgement and life in the new creation. There is no danger that people in the past or the present be considered mere means to the greater good of people in the future. The countless victims of history, those whose lives were torture and those who scarcely lived at all, are not to be forgotten, but remembered in hope of the resurrection.

For this metanarrative the past is not another country from which we have already travelled so far that it is of no more relevance to us. Knowing that all generations have a future in God's new creation, we practise solidarity with their sufferings, their achievements and their hopes, telling their stories as still relevant parts of the grand narrative of God's love for the world, past in which we may still find future. Not only the dead, but the living for whom there can be no more hope in this world, who can neither assist nor benefit from the onward march of progress – the desperately and incurably sick, the dying, the wretched of the earth – must not be left behind, but cherished with the special care God has for the most hopeless, since the future we cannot give them is promised them by God.

The horror, the tragedy and the loss, which are as much a part of history as fulfilment and achievement, have always – at least until certain modernist versions of Christianity – been fully acknowledged in the Christian metanarrative, since it is a narrative of redemption. The negatives of history – failure, wickedness, evil, suffering and death – require that history be redeemed as well as completed. The cross, where Jesus drank to the dregs the cup of God-forsaken death, is not a stage in the upward ascent of human history, but a descent to its depths in order to bring God into those depths. Since the cross cannot be edited out of the Christian metanarrative, it forbids those who tell the Christian story any whitewashing of history, any progressivist tale of success which neglects the victims, any of the glossy simulacra with which the image-makers of modernity mask the horrors of history.

The Christian metanarrative does not offer a speculative theodicy. It tells a story of God's dealings with evil which offers hope without minimizing or justifying evil. Above all, it finds in the cross God's loving solidarity with all who suffer and proffers hope for the end of history, when God will wipe away the tears from every eye and take his creation beyond the reach of evil. In the meantime the Christian story is open to all the cries and the protests of those who suffer. It does not silence them or explain them away, but allows them to keep the theodicy question agonizingly alive and open. By resisting premature closure, by keeping history open to the still future coming of God, Christian eschatology sustains our outrage against innocent and meaningless suffering.

No metanarrative, no story about the meaning of the whole of reality, can be trusted unless it is violently disrupted and threatened with contradiction of its meaning by the horrors of twentieth-century history. Therefore it is in the highest degree important not to tell the story as though it were an already completed whole. The sense of an ending impels us to seek the meaning of a story finally and fully only in the meaning given it by its end. The most satisfying fictional stories are those in which every part of the plot contributes to its resolution and all loose ends are finally tied up. But we know that such stories are unrealistic. Real life is full of aporias and discontinuities, randomness and dead ends, pointless suffering and waste. Only for the whole story of everything can we hope to encounter a real end which really gives meaning to the whole.

Such an end is not conceivable as a product of history, but only as a conclusion given by God, who will both complete and redeem the whole of history when he comes to end it. Christians trust God's promise that he will do this. But we cannot and should not attempt the reading of the whole of history that will be possible in the end. We discern God's providence in fragmentary ways, but we also encounter all the contradictions of meaning and purpose. The Christian metanarrative is open to all these, because it is still open to its conclusion.

A paradigm example in the biblical story is the massacre of the innocents (Matt. 2:16–18). Rachel, representing all the mothers of Bethlehem, her descendants, refuses consolation. Eschatologically her loss will be made good (Jer. 31:16–17), but just as Christian eschatology resists premature closure, so it refuses the premature consolation that pre-empts grief, the facile optimism which cannot recognize evil for what it is. The Christian story is not a completed unity, like a cosmic myth or a novel, but one in which we find ourselves. It is open to its own contradictions, which we experience as such and can transcend only in hope of an ending.

Eschatology's resistance to premature closure is important also in relation to the postmodernist suspicion of all metanarratives as oppressive and potentially violent, suppressing what is different and other in the name of what they falsely claim to be universal. The myth of progress has often proved oppressive in this way, but precisely because it demanded human achievement within history of properly eschatological goals. Attempts to achieve utopia are dangerous and often deadly. In distinction from the myth of progress, the indispensable element of transcendence in Christian eschatology forbids such utopianism. Where Christian totalizing violence exists – as it has done not infrequently in the history of the church – it has often been the result of prematurely realized eschatology.

The myth of progress sought to exorcize the terror of history – the future as unpredictable and uncontrollable – by mastering the future, thus in effect closing off the future in an extended and controllable present. Once again

Christian eschatology resists this kind of premature closure, keeping the future open to God's future. The future is not a linear extension of the past and the present – or, at least, is only made so by the myth of incremental progress. The future is the realm of open possibilities, which require evaluation and choice, and from which the genuinely and unpredictably new can arise. We can influence our future, but far from completely or predictably. We can neither master the future nor need wait passively for it (though this is sometimes required).

Christian hope is thus neither promethean nor quietist. It neither attempts what can only come from God nor neglects what is humanly possible. Sustained by the hope of everything from God, it attempts what is possible within the limits of each present. It does not overreach itself in striving for a post-historical goal. It does not value what can be done only as a step in a linear progress to a goal. It does what can be done for its own sake, here and now, confident that every present will find itself, redeemed and fulfilled, in the new creation.

Acknowledging human limits and taking seriously the transcendence of God thus go together. We exercise our responsibility within its properly human limits, and instead of aspiring disastrously to total control, we trust God. The open future is an invitation both to responsible action and to trust. The final future is an invitation to hope for the ultimately satisfying end that only God can give.

3

ᐤᐤᐤᐤᐤᐤᐤᐤᐤᐤ

The Wager on Transcendence: in Search of an Ecology of Hope

There is such a thing as an ecology of hope. There are environments in which it flourishes and others in which it dies.[1]

TRAGEDY AND TRANSCENDENCE

The story of hope in the western world is one which threatens to end tragically. Indeed, tragedy may well be the most appropriate literary genre with which to compare the story as it has played and is still playing itself out. The postmodern eschewal of story may itself ironically be construable as a tragic narrative denouement, a dark and despairing final scene in which dashed hopes, failed plans and unfulfilled promise litter the stage like corpses. A vision of ultimate meaninglessness; a mood of cosmic loneliness; an endurance of absolute and seemingly futile loss; an inability to see beyond the horizons of the present (itself inexorably shaped and determined by a past from which there is no final escape); an incapacity to imagine a future which is genuinely other than this present: the representation and evocation of these are among the defining characteristics of the tragic. The great paradox of tragedy lies in the fact that their evocation, skilfully handled by the writer, is actually the source of pleasure for

44

an audience, a pleasure contingent largely on the relative
detachment of the spectator from the action as such. 'As
we take pleasure in the representation of things that in
actual life we should find it painful and distressing to
watch, so we sympathize and admire persons whose acts
would in life shock and repel us.'[2] We participate in these
experiences, these moods, vicariously rather than directly.
Unlike the characters themselves we (together with the
actors) know that we shall be able to leave the theatre at
the end of the performance; and it is this tacit awareness
which enables us to find even satisfaction and consolation
in the tragic drama played out before us. It is not that we
do not consider the script or performance to be true to
reality, but simply that (for the time being at least) we are
able to transcend it, to walk away from the stark vision of
finitude and the questions lying at its boundaries with
which the action presents us. These same experiences and
moods, though, (or ones alarmingly like them) are the
forces which threaten to engulf our own society before
long under the guise of creeping apathy, indifference to
public concerns and even nihilism. In this context we are
no longer spectators but actors who cannot leave the stage.
This is not the skilful contrivance of great art but real life
and we discover that the 'tragedy'[3] looks different, is less
aesthetically pleasing, from where we have no choice but
to stand.

Where, then, in this figurative construal of recent history
ought we to look for the so-called 'tragic act' of which
such things are to be understood as the bitter fruit? In our
tale this role is played by the impassioned but unnatural
union between an emergent secular materialism and
classical Christian eschatology, an act of miscegenation
which duly spawned the modern myth of progress. No
doubt 'there was good sport at his making',[4] but the consequences of this particular bastard's veneration of Nature

and her laws are now apparent all around us. As an object or source of hope, the immanent goddess to which the myth of progress pays homage has not and will not now deliver the goods, even though she has received a good many sacrifices.

Those who pronounced the effective liberation of human life from divine rule and interference in the eighteenth century did so with the air of triumph attendant upon a great discovery. For them this was certainly not the end but the beginning of real hope. There is a sense in which, indeed, this intellectual shift consisted not so much in the abolition of deity as in its efficient relocation within the boundaries of immanence. 'God', to be sure, was no longer to be pictured as a powerful personal being over against and with ultimate responsibility for the destiny of creation; yet, as we have seen, belief in some overarching universal meaning and purpose in human existence, and in some intrinsic bias within the system towards the realization of that end, persisted. The vital difference was that this bias towards utopia was now thought of precisely as intrinsic, as a matter of natural evolution and human volition combined. The geography of heaven and earth had changed. 'God' was no longer 'up there' but 'in here', identified with the processes and principles of natural and human existence.

With what might well be described as God's second death, however, the mood is altogether different. The chilling words inscribed on the portals of Dante's Hell are displayed prominently above the entrance to the disillusionment of postmodernity.[5] As the pilgrim in Dante's tale observes, these are cruel words indeed. They apply now not to those whom God has rejected but to those who have rejected God: both the God of the Christian story *and* (after a lengthy probation) the deified principle substituted for God within the plot of the myth of progress.

46

There is no new contender for the position, no heir apparent to secure the succession. For, in a society whose imagination is bounded by purely immanent horizons, while modest local hopes may still be entertained and realized, there appears to be only one serious alternative to worshipping Nature as a source of *ultimate* or *cosmic* hope; namely, to face the spectres of meaninglessness, purposelessness and hopelessness.

In tragic art the observation of such deliberate 'facing' and endurance in others may produce a pleasure born of having glimpsed the depths of a shared and in some sense noble and dignified human condition.[6] The 'fascination with despair'[7] so characteristic of our late western culture (not least, worryingly, among the young) is, though, anything but ennobling or dignifying, threatening rather to dehumanize those caught in its grip. This suggests that the tragic vision ennobles precisely in so far as it reflects or evokes some level of *protest against* ultimate loss of meaning, that in allowing us, as it were, to peer over the edge into the formless void of Nothingness it stimulates in us a (perhaps subliminal) sense of the fundamental need for meaning, purpose, goodness, truth and beauty not as the arbitrary constructs of human convention, but as conditions of the physical, spiritual and moral universe within which human life is lived. Our humanity is affirmed not by embracing the loss of these, but in the pain which this same embrace causes. In its bid to liberate or distract us from such 'oppressive' concerns, encouraging temporary, superficial and irresponsible modes of response to the world ('Celebrate, play and enjoy, for tomorrow . . .'), the postmodern mood reveals itself to be an unsuitable host for the tragic, and therefore for hope. The distraction, like all anaesthetics, is limited in its effect and its duration. Before long, sharp twinges of reality remind us of the intensity of its true ache and, like Kent in the story of King Lear, we are driven back to the question 'Is *this* the promised end?'[8] While our postmodern minds may accept that it is thus, every other fibre in our humanity cries out with incredulity at this answer. We cannot in the end accept that this fruitless and desolate end (the close) of this story really reflects the end (the telos) of our shared existence. To do so would in effect be to deny the significance of that existence, and deep down we find this impossible to do.

The cost of God's second death, in other words, may finally be the loss of our essential humanity, a concession which many postmodern thinkers readily make, but one which most people appear to find it difficult to live in accordance with most of the time. All that we habitually identify as 'distinctively human' appears, when the matter is carefully weighed, to be contingent on the assumption of meaningfulness. This is true whether we are thinking, at one end of the scale, of that local meaningfulness which undergirds every communicative act of self-transcendence (the conversation with a friend or colleague, the interpretation of a text, a gesture, an action or a work of art), or, at the other, the overarching cosmic meaningfulness which pertains to questions of human hope. It will not suffice to appeal, as many postmodernists do, to the human capacity for invention and creativity as the source of all meaning, viewing truth, goodness, purposefulness and beauty as the local and conventional products of our poetic spontaneity.[9] As George Steiner observes, there are few deconstructionists among the poets and the artists in human society.[10] Those most 'creative' in the human community, that is to say, are precisely those who most vigorously resist the ascription of ultimate meaninglessness and formlessness to the world and its history. Their art, like the most basic and mundane linguistic exchanges, assumes the real presence of that which cannot in fact ever be demonstrated; namely, a meaningfulness which transcends the level of the symbolic and inheres in the nature of the real itself. Human creativity, artistic or otherwise, is never *ex nihilo*, but is a *response* to constant epiphanies through which reality impinges upon our existence. In the final analysis, Steiner insists, this 'wager' on the meaningfulness of meaning is precisely a wager on transcendence, on 'that in being which is not ours'.[11] In some sense, he suggests, it is a wager on 'God'.

What, though, of the meaningfulness of the human story as a whole? In this context the problem is precisely that so much of what we experience of life conflicts with that wager on meaning of which Steiner speaks. Yet our deepest intuitions, our gut feelings, resonate sympathetically with the wager. We protest against the horror of history and the concomitant terror which that horror inspires in us. The question is about how we should respond to these. The problem with the myth of progress was not its essential hopefulness, but rather its inability to deal with the way the world and we actually are, and the lack of any serious indication that things are either getting or going to get better. By mistakenly investing its faith in a glorious future which would grow naturally out of the conditions and potentialities of the present, therefore, the myth pointed to a meaningfulness which did not and could never exist within the terms of nature and history themselves. Its hope proved to be a false hope and so it had to come to an end, for false hopes inculcate only despair. It is to the credit of postmodernity that it has exposed the ideology of the myth. Yet its own essential hopelessness leaves us no better off, offering us only analgesic in place of false diagnosis. The raw nerve of pain which this unmasking of the myth exposes serves, though, to reinforce the question which comes so naturally to our humanity: is *this* the promised end?

In asking the question at all we already lean in the

direction of a negative answer to it. Yet if the human story is finally to be a comedy rather than a tragedy, then, it seems, it will have to be a *divina commedia*, and not one rooted in the natural ebb and flow of nature and history. It will have to be 'a fiction of improbable resolution',[12] and the improbability will be rooted in factors and possibilities lying beyond those apparent within the story itself. The immanent will not be able to drag itself by its own boot-straps out of the tragic mire which seems, according to all the evidence, to be the human lot. Here, then, we are forced to reckon with a 'wager on transcendence' of a distinct but directly related sort to that commended by Steiner. For we are not now concerned so much with a vertical transcendence, with a transcendent God whose way of being transcends ours and our world in the present moment, and whose existence underwrites the meaningful-ness which we trust even now lies beyond the flux and plurality of human perception and reflection. Instead, our wager is on a horizontal transcendence. That is, it is on a God who faithfully awaits us beyond the very end of history itself, whose capacities are such as to fashion out of our tragic endings (both individual and as a race) a future which wholly transcends the potential latent within history as such. Such a future is, in the ordinary run of things, wholly unlooked for and unpredictable, and even contra-dicts the patterns which we discern in the realm of nature and history.

Helen Gardner notes how, in art, it is perfectly permiss-ible for the tragedian, by presenting a dark and tormented vision of the human condition, to pose deep questions without any attempt to answer or resolve them. 'If there is any answer it lies in another world than the world of which the tragic poet presents an image.'[13] In pursuit of an answer to Kent's anguished inquiry, therefore, we must leave the stage where the tragedy is being played out and appeal to a wider vision of reality than its limited scenery allows us. We must finally transcend the tragic and make appeal to considerations lying beyond the purview of its drama. So too, it might be suggested, in our pursuit of a hopeful vision for humankind, we are forced finally to resort to an appeal beyond the boundaries of this tragic world, beyond this world and its intrinsic capacities altogether to another world, to indulge in a 'wager on transcendence' as the sole guarantor of ultimate meaning and purpose, the sole source of genuine hope.

Within the story which the Christian gospel tells about the destiny of our world just such a 'wager' is to be found. It is more familiarly referred to as faith in the God of the resurrection. While, therefore, Steiner's gambling metaphor has its appropriateness insofar as faith (like financial speculation) is an investment in something unseen and something which cannot, at the point of investment, be demonstrated to be true, nonetheless, within the logic of Christian faith the source of hope is one with very low odds indeed, if not a 'dead cert'! In faith, we shall see duly, our imagination is engaged, stretched and enabled to accommodate a vision of a meaningful and hopeful future for the world, a meaning which could never be had by extrapolating the circumstances of the tragic drama of history itself. The 'comic' ending is unlooked for, unexpected, improbable in the extreme whilever our imagination is constrained by the conditions of the immanent. Only by allowing our imagining to be blown wide open by a transcendence which blows the future itself wide open can we begin, however partially and tentatively, to envisage a *telos*, an end or purpose, which may legitimately furnish us with an object of hope. Recognition of this raises some important questions about just what sort of status may properly be ascribed to 'eschatological' language and the visions of transcendence to which it directs us. These will have to be addressed in due course. For now, though, there is more of a general nature to be said about hope and the ways in which it shapes human existence and ways of being in the world.

TO HOPE IS TO BE HUMAN

Hope is among those capacities or activities which mark off the territory of the distinctively human within our world. The quest for meaning, truth, goodness and beauty is closely bound up with hope as an activity of imagination in which we seek to transcend the boundaries of the present, to go beyond the given, outwards and forwards, in search of something more, something better, than the given affords us. Like Melville's Ishmael we are 'tormented with an everlasting itch for things remote',[14] not content with the given limits of our particularity. In this sense, as one writer puts the matter, '*Hope comes close to being the very heart and centre of a human being*'.[15] Humans, we might say, are essentially insatiable, driven forwards by a desire for contact with a reality the fullness of which constantly eludes us. Steiner's 'wager on transcendence' is, in this sense, precisely a hopeful venture: we step out in faith, trusting that there is something more, something better, something worthwhile, to be discovered or encountered, and that we shall duly be able to make contact with it. 'The truth is that the most fundamental and universal drive of man is toward objects, toward reality. We hope that we can reach this goal, we hope that there will be a response, physiological or psychological, from the world.'[16] From the simplest purposeful action (beginning with getting out of bed in the morning) to the most complex scientific, artistic or political engagement with the human condition, humanity lives not only by instinct and by desire but by hope. We live, that is to say, by stepping outwards and forwards from our present location in the hope that something positive will come of doing so, that such action is worthwhile. Such hope is usually bolstered by our experience of the past, but it is always determined equally by the inscrutable openness of the future with its attendant terrors. Hope is a matter of both knowledge and will (we know what has happened before, and we know what we desire) but it is characterized above all by the application of imagination and trust to a future which is essentially open and unknown. With its eyes wide open to the threat which the future holds, it nonetheless sees ways of averting this threat. Hope is, in this sense, an activity of imaginative faith.

In his magisterial study of the nature of language and translation, *After Babel*, George Steiner observes the impact of grammar upon this vectorial dimension of human existence. 'The status of the future of the verb,' he writes, 'is at the core of existence. It shapes the image we carry of the meaning of life, and of our personal place in that meaning.'[17] 'We move forwards in the slipstream of the statements we make about tomorrow morning.'[18] Our capacity to move forwards, to transcend the givenness of the present is, in other words, closely tied to our capacity to speak the future into existence, to fashion an imagined tomorrow or next year and to bring it to expression. Through the imaginative construction and projection of what Steiner dubs 'axiomatic fictions' with respect to the future we are, as it were, drawn forward in their wake and live towards tomorrow rather than being absorbed by a closed and hopeless present. Conversely, possession of a future tense is the preserve of those who are able to imagine otherwise, to envisage the possibility of change; to hope. Of course, imagination is also the source of fear, whether pathological or well-founded; but, as we have suggested, fear and hope are not necessary opposites. Hope is not rooted in an air-brushing of difficulty out of the picture, but in an imagining of the future which envisages ways of flourishing in spite of genuine dangers and threats. Thus, Steiner suggests, it is among the distinguishing characteristics of humans to be hopeful, to be directed towards the future in all its openness and *despite* its terrors. It is no accident, he avers, that the species we know to possess a highly developed set of languages should also be found at the top of the evolutionary tree. Imagination and hope, which are closely tied to our ability to speak the future, are capacities which fit us for survival. 'The conventions of forwardness so deeply entrenched in our syntax make for a constant, sometimes involuntary, resilience. Drown as we may, the idiom of hope, so immediate to the mind, thrusts us to the surface.'[19] 'Natural selection has favoured the subjunctive.'[20]

This account concurs with that of the Jesuit writer William Lynch who, in a lengthy consideration of hope, imagination and mental health, describes hope as a constant decision to move into the future, a bid to transcend the present with its perceived limits and difficulties, to imagine a way out of that which constrains and threatens to engulf or imprison us into a brighter and better alternative. Thus, hope is that which insists on expanding our perceived horizons of possibility, broadening the landscape of reality in such a way as to set our present circumstance in a wider perspective and thereby to rob it of its absoluteness. Even in the most difficult and threatening of situations hope 'is always slow to admit that all the facts are in, that all the doors have been tried, and that it is defeated'.[21]

Hope, in such an account of things, is essentially liberating and invigorating with respect to our present existence. Hope transfigures every empirical present by relating it to a vision of the future. It is vital to state this clearly, for where religious hope has received a bad press it has often been due to a misperception of it as an essentially quietistic and other-worldly attitude which robs us of the will to struggle against various ills in this world. This, of course, was the analysis offered by Karl Marx with respect to religious hope. His description of religion as 'the opiate of the people' correctly identified the power of hope over our ways of being in the present, but misconstrued its essential dynamic. For Marx religion is a cosmic aspirin, an analgesic deliberately administered by the rich and powerful to dull the pain of the workers' lot and thereby prevent the otherwise inevitable eventual reaction to sustained injustice, exploitation and deprivation. Visions of an other-worldly future, Marx assumes, are effective in numbing the oppressed masses to the dark reality of hell on earth. They render us too heavenly-minded to be of any earthly (political) use. Our argument thus far has suggested that while this diagnosis may well apply to the virtual realities mass-produced and peddled on the postmodern market, it misses the essential point of Christian hope.

As we shall see duly, there is a proper and vital sense in which Christian hope is invested in the imagination of the 'other-worldly'; but to construe it as quietistic is wholly to misrepresent its intentions. As Christian theologian Jürgen Moltmann observes:

> Faith, wherever it develops into hope, causes not rest but unrest, not patience but impatience. It does not calm the unquiet heart, but is itself this unquiet heart in man. Those who hope in Christ can no longer put up with reality as it is, but begin to suffer under it, to contradict it. Peace with God means conflict with the world, for the goad of the promised future stabs inexorably into the flesh of every unfulfilled present.[22]

Moltmann's view of religious hope stands Marx's on its head and insists that the imaginative capacity of such hope to reach beyond the limits and lacks of the present, far from paralysing protest, actually furnishes the fuel which drives political will and is the ultimate source of all genuine protest against the given. Only insofar as we are able to envisage how things might be different from the way they are in this world, how they might change in the future, how they are intended by God ultimately to be, do we have any final grounds for refusing to accept the way the world presently is. In other words, the 'utopia' proper to Christian eschatology offers no less than its Marxist alternative in this respect.

At this level, therefore, Christian hope may properly be considered one version of a shared human phenomenon. So Ernst Bloch, on whose encyclopaedic analysis of the forms which hope takes and the roles which it plays in human life Moltmann draws, writes in similar vein: 'The pull towards what is lacking never ends. . . . The lack of what we dream about hurts not less, but more. It thus prevents us from getting used to deprivation.'[23] Hope transfigures the present precisely by enabling us to transcend it imaginatively and, upon our return, to perceive all too clearly its lacks and needs. According to the popular proverb 'You don't miss what you have never had'. But to imagine is, for all practical purposes, already to have had, to have tasted the fruit which lies beyond, to have one's appetite for the possible thoroughly whetted so that the actual begins to taste sour by comparison. Soon hope begins to devise strategies for escape.

In truth it is a pathological lack of hope, hopelessness (a condition which Lynch identifies as symptomatic of many forms of mental illness) which saps our energy and imprisons us within the tyranny of an absolute present. A serious failure of imagination renders us incapable of transcending the apparent limits of the here and now. With quite literally nothing to look forward to ('No future for you and me!' as one classic punk-rock lyric has it) we have little choice but to adjust to a cyclical pattern in which the same old dead-end options present themselves with a sickening regularity, each inviting just one more exploration which we know perfectly well will end in the brick wall of impossibility and failure.

In our own society this hopelessness is worryingly apparent. Overwhelmed by the enormity of the ideology of indeterminacy and relativism (epistemic, moral, aesthetic, religious), crushed by the thought of ultimate Nothingnessness (of which, as Lear reminds us, nothing ever comes[24]), having had its hopes temporarily raised by the myth of progress only to see them dashed again, the West has for some decades been presenting symptoms of corporate stress disorder. The social body, drained of energy and enthusiasm by two and a half centuries of strenuous effort chasing impossible goals, lies exhausted, its get up and go having long since got up and gone. A deep-rooted sense of ultimate meaninglessness is having practical knock-on effects in everyday and local contexts. The sphere of private interest expands constantly at the expense of concern for an identifiable common good and projects designed to facilitate it. The death of truth threatens to lead inexorably to the death of human culture in the sense of 'a creative project in which human beings have an ethical, artistic and political role to play'.[25] No one, it seems, wants to be bothered very much any more with anything or anyone else. There is a loss of any serious sense of public accountability or concern, a fact reflected on the one hand in the relatively small proportion of enfranchised citizens who choose actually to vote in local and national ballots, and on the other in the increasing number who appear to be prepared to resort to anti-social and even violent forms of protest and direct action in order to see their own chosen values prevail.

The perception that there is no exit, no way forward, nothing that can be done, may in the short term provoke a frenzied hyperactivity in which we seek to stave off our fears of what may be (about which nothing can be done) by immersing ourselves wholly in the pleasures, benefits and distractions which the present has to offer. This may take the form of sheer narcotic hedonism (indulging in sensory excess 'like there's no tomorrow') or a wholesale investment of our concern in artificial, contrived and illusory goals and projects. What is effectively a process of denial cannot last, however, and eventually gives way to a deeper and more lasting inertia and a sense of aimlessness and futility.

Thus, not wanting to be bothered with a despairing shared world, we postmodern individuals retreat instead into our private televisual and computerized virtual realities which, unlike the 'real world', we can programme, control and edit to our own advantage and personal delight. Instead of sharing in community we now prefer to face not other people but the monitor, logging into a cyber-personal internet which grants us hitherto unimaginable access to a vast electronic cosmos, but which, ironically, simultaneously divorces us from flesh and blood reality itself. The alternative postmodern cosmos of cyber-space recreates momentarily the frisson of that power which the myth of progress institutionalized, fostering 'the delusion of the frontier mentality while implying that you can get (whatever) you want by simply pressing a button'.[26] It is not lack of imagination that is the problem here, therefore: on the contrary, the postmodern ethos of play is all about the 'cathartic power to make what is impossible at the empirical level of existence possible at the symbolic level'.[27] But such imagining has no aspiration to transcendence, no forward moving and potentially liberating direction. It is deployed only as a narcotic, to substitute various virtual alternatives for reality, fictional possibilities designed to satisfy our unnaturally circumscribed desire and so distract us (for the time being) from the actual impossibilities and futility of life.

Meanwhile, as we are reminded each time we log out of cyberspace and our colourful simulations fade, the anxiety-inducing contours of our shared history remain the same. Indeed, every retreat into individualistic fantasy threatens simply to reinforce them by diverting the vital resources of energy and effort which might otherwise make some small but intrinsically worthwhile difference. Postmodern imagination is, in this sense, distinctly unethical. It fosters a sense of alienation from a public world which is, after all, a social construct which I may choose either to endorse and participate in or not. As Richard Kearney observes, one of the most serious symptoms of the postmodern failure of imagination is the likely eventual loss of the other, the one who confronts us and who places us under some irreducible ethical obligation as fellow human beings.[28] After all, if there is no ultimate meaning, no final truth, if nothing is really real, then it is possible to ignore with impunity the piercing eyes of the starving child or the bewildered refugee whose face is beamed across the globe into our private space by satellite TV, or to turn a blind eye to the mugging or the racist attack taking place on our own doorstep. Such things, we might come to suppose, are not our proper concern and should not be allowed to spoil our day. So we draw the curtains or reach for the remote channel changer. We can't be bothered to act because such action would draw us out of our individual privacy into a complicating set of relationships which would be inconvenient and costly and which would in the end, we suppose, make very little difference to anything.

When the need of the other ceases to meet with any deep response in us in this way, when we are able to satisfy our innate craving for contact with the real through the breath-taking (but ultimately prophylactic) simulacra of 'virtual reality', when our ethical sensibility is massaged through vicarious identification with larger than life Hollywood heroes but we cannot actually face the comparatively small responsibilities which real life occasionally thrusts in our face, we can be sure that the question of the erosion of our humanity itself has become deadly serious. 'What could I have done? What real difference would it have made?' These are the questions with which the apathy born of hopelessness justifies itself, before turning its back on the whole despairing scene and rejoining one or another virtual alternative which calls it to *do* precisely nothing except sit back and prepare to be entertained to death. We are living, one contemporary lyric complains, in a plastic world in which the fresh air of reality is barely perceptible through the thick perfume of illusion, illusion which we are not even free to choose or create for ourselves (although of course we live under the *illusion* that we are!) but which must be selected from a range of products carefully imposed by the totalitarianism of the 'free' market:

> The world is turning Disney and there's nothing you can do
> You're trying to walk like giants, but you're wearing Pluto's
>   shoes. . . .
> And the answers fall easier from the barrel of a gun
> Than it does from the lips of the beautiful and the dumb
> The world won't end in darkness, it'll end in family fun
> With Coca Cola clouds behind a Big Mac sun[29]

Meanwhile the forces of cynicism, paranoid self-interest and active nihilism (in both their individual and their corporate forms) stalk the world's stage with less and less to oppose their advance.

The net result of hopelessness is thus precisely to change nothing except, perhaps, insofar as it allows things to get even worse. This, in turn, serves to reinforce the original sense of impossibility and locks the hopeless ever more securely into the vicious and downward spiral of denial and despair in which so much imaginative energy is expended in doing nothing and going nowhere. The following exchange between Samuel Beckett's two victims of late modern indeterminacy, Vladimir and Estragon, captures the mood:

Vladimir:	(*without anger*) It's not certain.
Estragon:	No, nothing is certain.
. . . .	
Estragon:	It's not worth while now.
	Silence.
Vladimir:	No, it's not worth while now.
	Silence.
Estragon	Well, shall we go?
Vladimir:	Yes, let's go.
	They do not move.[30]

As a self-proclaimed culture of hopelessness postmodernity is in danger of just such inertia. It is a condition without a sense of the future, and as such, no matter how much activity it may generate within the 'labyrinth of endless play'[31] which is its own absolutized present, it is going nowhere. Incapable of relevant acts of imaginative self-transcendence, having officially abandoned belief in the existence of a way out of the labyrinth or a golden thread to lead us there, it is threatened with the loss of its own humanity.

61

HOPE FOR THE HOPELESS

Not all hopelessness is bad for us, let alone dehumanizing. Hopelessness can be a perfectly healthy condition and, correspondingly, hope may be pathological. In this world there are hopes which crush as well as hopes which liberate. It all depends how well founded our hope proves to be. Hope has its legitimate limits, and it is vital that we identify them correctly lest we mistakenly invest ourselves in a dead end, an option with no future. Otherwise we shall live for a time with dangerous illusions the eventual unmasking of which will be all the more painful and damaging to our mental well-being.

In his careful analysis of this subject Lynch reminds us that hope is no mere heroic subjective disposition of the individual, an attitude which, regardless of what faces it, soldiers on, refusing to accept defeat long after the battle has been lost, convinced that through its striving and contrivance things may yet be turned around. Real hope is far less focused on its own capabilities. It is not concerned with some supposed right or capacity to choose and to create for itself the reality which it desires. Real hope is essentially rooted in the qualities and capacities of otherness, of that which lies beyond itself in other people, in the 'real world'. It is, in Lynch's words, 'an interior sense that there is help on the outside of us'.[32] Hope is a hunch about what is genuinely possible. It is rooted in an intuitive judgement about the help which lies at hand. In Steiner's sense it is a wager on transcendence, on something which lies beyond us, as yet unseen but, we believe, real enough. Here is another reason for postmodernity's inability to hope. Hope does not fit well into a predominantly individualistic DIY culture of self-sufficiency in which 'reality' is deemed to come (in some sense) from resources to be discovered within, where what lies beyond us is a gallery

62

of images and simulations, and in which suspicion, not trust, is everyone's ultimate watchword. Hope knows it needs help, and it thinks it knows where to find it.

The difference between true and false hope may thus be deemed to be that the one gets this judgement right and the other gets it wrong. Ernst Bloch insists upon a distinction between the proper imaginative activity of hope on the one hand and what he calls 'mere fantasizing' on the other. In the former, hope as a component of human consciousness (a hopeful disposition) is soundly rooted in real possibilities in the world, even when the means for or route to realizing these may not yet be at all apparent. Hope intuits 'a Not-Yet-Being of an expectable kind'.[33] It is not a matter of easy prediction, for hope is often a stretching of the imagination way beyond the limits of what is currently possible; but hope, as opposed to mere fantasizing, attaches itself to a 'Real-Possible', some set of circumstances the conditions for the possibility of which are genuinely present within the conditions and possibilities of the here-and-now. It is the conviction that this is so which drives hope forward towards its own eventual realization, struggling to overcome what may seem to be insuperable obstacles in the process. We keep going, keep striving to find a way forward precisely because we believe there is such a way even when we cannot yet see it clearly. Imagination fuels the engines of our movement into the future. Mere fantasizing, on the other hand, is a matter only of projecting our desires on to the blank screen of what may lie beyond. Nothing is intuited; there is no serious wager on transcendence; we are simply entertaining ourselves in the meanwhile. Such fantasizing has no liberating potential. It is, as we have already seen, a diversion from facing up to reality and can only last so long before its illusion fades and needs to be replaced by another. Finally it binds us ever more securely within the

confines of a limited and despairing present. Real hope
liberates and moves us forward. False hope entraps and
leaves us, listless, essentially where we began.

Imagination, Lynch suggests, may be either artistic or
neurotic. The artist, through imaginative self-transcendence, opens up for us visions of reality (including its
possible futures) through a creative wager on transcendence, and thereby actually helps 'to invent the future of
man and to extend man's possibilities'.[34] Neurotic imagination confines our thoughts and feelings through the
ideological imposition of (artificial) limits on the landscape of reality. Postmodernity does this first through the
totalitarian imposition of indeterminacy and the subsequent marketing of a range of alternative virtual realities
for our indwelling. Thereby it crushes our capacity for
genuine hope precisely in order to make room for hopes
of a false or illusory sort. In the postmodern world our
desires, and thereby our patterns of behaviour, are carefully controlled by those whom we allow to create 'reality'
for us, who, through the manipulation and marketing of
images, form our imagining and shape our desire.

Perhaps, though, at the end of the twentieth century we
owe postmodernity a certain debt of gratitude at least for
its exposure of the ideology of progress. This ideology was,
in the sense we have been considering, precisely a false
hope, offering an illusory future which has finally faded
before our eyes. Our liberation from it can only be considered a good thing since, as Lynch argues, where there
is no genuine possibility of help, where we are not confronted with a Real-Possible, a certain sort of hopelessness
(i.e. a sober recognition of our limits, a facing of the
realities of our situation) is actually the most healthy attitude to adopt. Identification of the difference between
what is possible for us in this world and what is not is of
the essence of human well-being.

The problem with which postmodernity burdens us is that of an almost all-embracing hopelessness. Not everything is possible for us in this world; but many things are, and these may legitimately furnish objects of hope to which we can look and move forward. Even if our goals and projects are of limited scope and relatively small scale (the grand utopia of the myth having been unmasked as an illusion) they are nonetheless in themselves perfectly good and proper things towards which to work. Their value as objects of hope, that is to say, is not tied to a perception of them as successful steps towards utopia. But postmodernity seems to have allowed (or to be threatening to allow) its cosmic hopelessness to trickle down through the entirety of human existence, robbing its adherents of the energy and will even to move towards small-scale and short-term goals. This suggests that the stability of hope *within* history may finally prove to be contingent upon the existence of some hope *for* history, that penultimate and small-scale hopes are difficult if not impossible to sustain where no firm basis for an ultimate and cosmic hope exists. It's like reading some novels: prior warning that the ending is a poor one drains our enthusiasm for the remaining chapters. We may as well expend our energy and attention in some other way.

Is such a final hope, belief in a 'good ending', any longer possible for humanity? Not if we seek to root it in the soil of modern or postmodern ideologies. Neither of these is capable of sustaining an 'ecology of hope' for reasons which we have seen. Their failure to do so does not, of course, in itself do anything to render the broad outlines of Christian hope inherently believable, let alone demonstrate their truth. Perhaps, though, it at least gives pause for thought and raises the question whether a careful reconsideration of the imaginative resources of Christian eschatology is not overdue. After all, what is to be lost in such a venture? And, as we have seen, the stakes otherwise are high ones. Our humanity itself may be under threat. If, as Bloch, Steiner, Lynch and others suggest, the condition of hope is in some sense essential to that humanity then the failure of 'humanity come of age' to discover adequate moorings for hope (which is to put the matter mildly!) presents a serious problem. Is the perennial human quest for meaning, truth, goodness and beauty (the project of hope) simply a sick joke played on us by an essentially amoral and value-free evolutionary process? Is an inability to rest content with a negative answer to this question itself arbitrary? Or does it point to some deficiency in the diagnosis?

It is certainly incumbent upon Christians, in a context where such questions have become urgent, to return to their tradition and familiarize themselves with its distinctive stock of images and ways of imagining the future, and to make these available in intelligent contemporary versions for public consideration. No doubt they will also welcome and be willing to listen to other voices, religious or otherwise, who have significant contributions to make to the discussion. When this task is undertaken it will become clear that the Christian story (if its truth be entertained as a hypothesis) does afford a route beyond the impasse, an exit from the labyrinth of postmodern despair, an environment in which an ecology of hope may flourish; and it does so precisely by virtue of its own peculiar 'wager on transcendence'.

Wilfred Owen's poem 'Futility' gives voice to the innate human incredulity in the face of the apparent finality of death:

> Move him into the sun –
> Gently its touch awoke him once,
> At home, whispering of fields unsown.

. . . .
Think how it wakes the seeds, –
Woke, once, the clays of a cold star.
Are limbs, so dear-achieved, are sides,
Full-nerved – still warm – too hard to stir?
Was it for this the clay grew tall? . . .

In the libretto of Benjamin Britten's *War Requiem* these
words (and others like them) are juxtaposed provocatively
with extracts from Christian liturgy. The poet's tortured
closing inquiry, 'O what made fatuous sunbeams toil/ To
break earth's sleep at all?', is met with the ancient invo-
cation 'all pitying Lord Jesus, grant them rest,' and set
within the wider context of prayers for eternal light and
the transition from death to life promised to Abraham
and his seed.

The tension generated by this simple juxtaposition
points us to the source from which Christian hope for the
world and its future wells up, and from which all local
tributaries of hope and energy for action ultimately flow.
The apostle Paul, alluding to his experiences of persecution in Asia, writes: 'we felt that we had received the
sentence of death so that we would rely not on ourselves
but on God who raises the dead'.[35] This sums the matter
up nicely. The point is that the tragic dimensions of human
life cannot and will not be resolved within the boundaries
of either history or nature. Neither the most advanced
technologies or ingenious human projects nor the sun's
warming and otherwise life-giving rays can address the
futile loss to which the poet bears witness. And in this
respect our personal mortality stands as a profound symbol
of the wider reaches of death and its dark forces in human
life. If this is true at the level of our individual finitude
then it is all the more so in relation to the meaningfulness
and fulfilment of the human story as a whole. If this story

is to have a comic rather than a tragic ending then, Christian faith recognizes, it will only be through the contrivance of the God of the resurrection, the God who is able to bring life out of death, being out of non-being, that all is resolved well and everything finally works together for good.

We shall, in other words, have at the last to be rescued (a metaphor to which the commonly used but less commonly carefully used language of 'salvation' itself directs us) from the shipwreck of history by one who stands outside its horizons. Nothing within the possibilities and potentialities of nature or history considered in themselves could account for a more than tragic ending to the human story. However laudable and good in themselves many of the achievements of humankind may be, rearranging the deckchairs on the *Titanic* and calling it a new way forward, a new world order, or whatever, will not actually melt the iceberg of finitude on which our dreams and hopes seem bound to run aground. For imagination constrained by the limited possibilities of immanence, therefore, it seems that there is little genuine hope to be had. But within the logic of Christian faith it is not the possibilities of the finite in which we are called to invest our trust, but rather the God with and for whom all things are possible. Precisely how the world will end is, of course, something which in the strictest sense lies currently beyond our imagining; but faith is nurtured, as we shall see, by a rich stock of images in terms of which to imagine the unimaginable: A world with no more war, no more suffering, no more death, no more loss. A world in which all the unfulfilled potential of history will somehow be taken up into fulfilment, all losses made good, all injustices set to rights. A world in which the hegemony of death will at last be broken open and swallowed up in the establishment of life in all its fullness.

It is thus by an imaginative appeal of hope beyond the

limits of the historical and the natural that Christian faith is evoked and sustained. Faith in the God and Father of Jesus Christ is faith in the God who raised Jesus from the dead, an action which while it is certainly presented as having occurred within history must equally certainly be admitted to lie beyond the range of possibilities of history as such. In this respect the resurrection of Jesus is the paradigm case for Christian hope, and its essential dynamic is mirrored in many other scriptural accounts and features of Christian experience. It is, like Christian faith itself in John's account of it as 'new birth',[36] 'from above', not to be accounted for in purely human or historical terms. It arises out of the intervention of God in the midst of the here and now. It is in the world, but not of the world. As Moltmann suggests,[37] the relationship between the crucified Jesus and the risen Lord must therefore furnish the gestalt for imagining the relationship between the tragic limits of this world and the surprising, comic dimensions of God's new creation. This latter image speaks of the rupture-in-the-midst-of-continuity between the old and the new. 'See,' says God in his final speech in the Bible, 'I am making all things new'.[38] All things will not *become* new through some natural process or human programme of works, but must be *made* new: made new, that is to say, by the same creator God who made them in the beginning and who graciously holds them in existence from moment to moment. Thus this is a genuine newness which wholly transcends the state of the here and now with its tragic limits, yet which does not collapse into a novelty in which this creation is no longer the object of God's concern and action, having effectively been abandoned and replaced by another.

It should be clear that the primary horizon of this hope is in the future. The new creation, that is to say, has not yet occurred, and when it does it will involve a radical refashioning of the very foundations of the cosmos as we know it, an event the implications of which we can only begin to imagine. But this does not render Christian hope empty of present significance, as if it were a matter of sitting back and waiting for God to step in and call down the final curtain on history. As we have already seen, genuine hope has the capacity to transfigure our perception and experience of the present, and to transform our ways of being in the world. So it is with Christian faith, which is above all things forward looking and forward moving. To be a Christian might be defined as living in the light cast by the resurrection; living, that is to say, as those who insist on interpreting this world in terms of its (surprising and unexpected) future as made known to us in the resurrection of Jesus by his Father in the power of the Holy Spirit. It is in this sense that Christian hope is properly 'other-worldly'. Here we might venture the view that in this regard it is able to do what Marx's utopia cannot, the latter finally offering an inadequate diagnosis of and prescription for the human condition.

Meanwhile, though, there is more even than this to be said. For it is a vital part of a Christian perspective on this world to identify within it scattered acts of recreative anticipation of God's promised future, as the same Spirit who raised Jesus from death calls into being life, health, faith and hope where there is otherwise no capacity for these and no accounting for them. Such anticipations are to be found *in* this world, but they are not *of* this world in the sense of having identifiable and sufficient natural antecedents in it. They belong to God's future of which they are heralds and towards which they direct our hopeful gaze. In such happenings the power of the future-made-present is manifest, the lustre of the new creation shines provocatively from behind the heavy clouds of history. In the meanwhile Christians are called to identify and to become involved with God's Spirit in all that he is doing to fashion a genuine presence of the new within the midst of the old, drawing it into self-transcendent albeit partial anticipations of what it will ultimately be. Thus hope is a dynamic affair; it involves us inevitably in a struggle with the principalities and powers of this world, a struggle in which ironically we are liberated from fear and guilt by the knowledge that in and of ourselves we cannot win; yet we are encouraged by the equally firm conviction that with the God and Father of Jesus Christ all things are possible, and he has promised to make all things new.

If the crucifixion-resurrection of Jesus is the paradigm for the Christian's eschatological expectation then in some sense we must suppose ourselves as people of hope to be located on that day of which Scripture tells us nothing whatsoever: Easter Saturday.[39] This day is bounded on the one side by all the horror of history symbolically concluded in the events of Good Friday, and on the other by the open future of God who raises the dead to life on the dawn of Easter Sunday. In the meanwhile we live and travel in hope, able to face squarely and in all their awfulness the horrific aspects of that history within whose temporal boundaries we actually still live precisely and only because the terror of history no longer haunts us. Instead, through the captivity of our imagination, God's Spirit draws us forward into the reality of his own future, a future the openness of which is no longer a threat, therefore, but a source of that joyful energy under the influence of which God calls us, for now, to live and labour in the world.

4

ooooooooooo

Ambiguous Vision: Hope, Imagination and the Rhetoric of the Unsayable

Flesh and blood cannot inherit the kingdom of God, nor does the perishable inherit the imperishable.

(1 Cor. 15:50)

Hope, we have suggested, is a vital function of imagination lying at the heart of our humanity. Specifically, it is the capacity to imagine otherwise, to transcend the boundaries of the present in a quest for something more, something better, than the present affords. Christianity is above all a tradition characterized by hope. It is forward looking with respect both to this world and the next, and its hope is invested in the capacities and promises of the God made known in Jesus' death and resurrection. This same God draws us, by faith, out of the patterns of sin and death which mark our past and present, and into his own future of which resurrection is both the sign and the pledge.

THE CERTAINTY OF THINGS NOT SEEN?

To acknowledge hope as an imaginative enterprise, though, has immediate implications for the ways in which we approach and understand the forms in which, in Scripture and elsewhere, the Christian hope is characteristically

72

expressed. When Christians speak of God's future, in other words, what *sorts* of statements are they making? How is language being used here? And how, therefore, should we treat such statements? For the purposes of convenience, we may begin by presenting what is admittedly an over-stated and crude analysis of two different ways in which eschatological statements (statements about the 'last things' or *eschata*) might be and often have been understood.

The first of these ways treats eschatological statements as possessed of directly predictive force, as straightforwardly descriptive of states of affairs which will actually come to pass in due course. On this view, biblical accounts of the hereafter afford Christians a sort of sneak preview of the future, a quick glance at the last chapter of God's dealings with humankind and the cosmos from which suf-ficient facts, figures and other bits of information may be garnered for us to be able to speak with confidence about the basic shape and content of the ultimate future. In his *City of God* the fourth-century African theologian Augustine offers a good example of one such approach when he engages in a careful and sustained reflection on the ques-tion of whether it will be possible for the bodies of those in hell to be burned by the fires there in such a way that, while they feel the pain proper to such burning, they are not actually consumed by the flames, the torments of hell having properly to be eternal rather than temporary.[1] The tone both of his questions and the answers which he prof-fers assume what I shall argue is an overly 'literal' or factual interpretation of eschatological language, one which func-tions by extending the conditions and potentialities of the here-and-now into the hereafter. It operates, that is to say, with an inverted form of the so-called historicist 'principle of analogy', constructing its view of the future on the basis of what is known to be actual, probable and possible

73

in experience of the present.² Thus, Augustine refers his readers to a fascinating freak-show of this-worldly phenomena in which proximity to fire does not appear to result in combustion. His purpose in doing so is precisely to establish the credibility of a (revealed) 'fact' about the next world, and to defend it thereby from pagan derision.

The second of our two types of approach would not dream of asking (what it would consider to be) such crude questions, let alone of attempting to answer them. It construes eschatological statements as essentially poetic rather than factual or scientific in kind, and does not invest them with any serious intent to describe or to communicate 'information' about the future at all. Thus, while biblical visions of, for example, God's new creation or the kingdom of God may tell us a good deal about the political or spiritual aspirations, values and desires of the individuals and communities from which they sprang, or be interpreted as symbolic commentaries on the writers' and original readers' present, they were never intended and cannot in fact tell us anything reliable about the future (let alone the far-flung future of the eschaton) at all. To take them as if they could is to commit a basic category or genre error, and to risk deluding ourselves in ways which can only rob us of a proper grasp on the reality of our circumstance in the here-and-now. This is the view made popular in the middle of the twentieth century by the German New Testament scholar and theologian Rudolf Bultmann. Eschatological language, Bultmann insists, together with much else in the New Testament, is to be classified as 'myth', a way of clothing general features of the human condition in imaginative form in order vividly to express the truth about them. Thus, language about the kingdom of God, the end of the world, the last judgement, and so on, is properly to be understood as a mythological way of speaking not about the future at all, but about the present. Specifically, 'it says to men that this present world, the world of nature and history, the world in which we live our lives and make our plans is not the only world; that this world is temporal and transitory, yes, ultimately empty and unreal in the face of eternity.'[3] Such myths, properly understood, attempt to tell us nothing about the future of this world or its eventual destiny. Their concern is with drawing attention to aspects of the present, and hence with changing the way in which we think about and behave in it.

There are problems attaching to the logic of our talk about the future in general, and the content of Christian hope in particular, which render the first of these two approaches untenable. In interpreting talk about the future, our willingness to invest it with reliable indicative intent or achievement is generally tied directly to its relation to the continuities of the past and the present as we know and experience (or have known and experienced) these, or believe them to be (or have been). On the whole, that is to say, we do apply some version of the principle of analogy, assuming that, in broad terms, the future is likely to be similar in shape to the past and the present. Thus, a statement which we make about tomorrow or the week after next ('On 27th November I shall leave San Francisco and fly back to the UK') is likely to be evaluated in terms of its fundamental consonance with what we believe to be true about the present (I have a ticket, I have no legally binding engagements in San Francisco on November 28th, and so on), and the extrapolation of relationships and continuities of order drawn from our experience of the past (the 27th November will actually follow the 26th again this year as it always has done previously, 'I' will be the same person on November 27th as I am today, and so on). There are, of course, contingencies which may serve to produce a quite different outcome. My flight may be cancelled. I may meet an untimely end under the wheels of a San Francisco tram. Such things are possible. 'Factual' or indicative statements about the future are, in the ordinary run of things, therefore, never absolutely certain; and when we make such statements ('I am going to get my hair cut this afternoon', 'There will be a solar eclipse in three months' time', 'The universe will eventually return to the oblivion out of which it came in the big bang') a lesser degree of certainty attaches to our speech than pertains to other assertions we might make ('The First World War ended on November 11th 1918', 'It rained heavily yesterday', 'I have a headache'). The further forwards from the present our statements reach, we might suppose, the more room there will be for contingencies of various sorts to interfere with our intentions or calculations, and the less certain our assertions must be judged to be.

Those wishing to adhere to more literal or direct readings of eschatological language may be expected to appeal at this point to the category of revelation in support of their cause. After all, a 'revelation' is precisely a manifestation of something which would otherwise remain hidden or obscure. Could it not be argued, then, that in biblical eschatology we are dealing with just such a surprising but real divulging of factual secrets about the shape and content of the end towards which history is moving? One sort of response to this would have to be couched in terms of a careful consideration of literary genre, and the suggestion that the relevant biblical materials themselves would not have been understood by their writers or their first readers as an attempt to chart the history of the future. Here, though, we shall pursue a different sort of consideration which has its point of departure in the content of Christian hope itself.

'BEHOLD I AM DOING A NEW THING'

The Christian hope is finally invested not in an extension of or a development from the conditions, actualities and potentialities of the present order of things, but in a decisive activity of the God who in the beginning called this same order into being out of nothing, and who promises us a transformation of our situation so radical as to be pictured under the figure of a wholly new creative act on God's part.

One way of approaching the significance of this is through consideration of the term 'new' in biblical prophecy and apocalypse. The relevant Hebrew word (*chadash*), like its English counterpart, has to bear several senses. It can refer simply to another of the same kind. So, for example, a 'new' king (Ex. 1:8) is just the next king in a succession of kings. But the same word can also designate the qualitatively new, the unprecedented, the new which utterly surpasses the old. Greek has the advantage here of possessing two words (*neos* and *kainos*), of which *kainos* refers more naturally or properly to the qualitatively new. This distinction is not consistently observed in the New Testament usage, but it holds to quite a large extent.

Our culture has become addicted to constant trivial novelty and wearily accustomed to the assumption that the new is always better, a modernist prejudice hijacked by commercialism. Newness has become so banal that it is hard for us to appreciate the force of the concept of the qualitatively new in biblical literature. Perhaps we need first to hear again the disillusioned observation of the Preacher in *Ecclesiastes* that 'there is nothing new under the sun. Is there a thing of which it is said, "See, this is new"? It has already been in the ages before us' (Eccles. 1:9–10). This dulling sense of the fundamental sameness of human history and experience highlights for us all the

more those passages in the prophets which speak of something genuinely new even by the Preacher's exacting
standards, acts of God which will so exceed the ordinary
course of things as to amount to a new creation. Unlike
ourselves, the biblical writers are actually quite sparing in
their use of the term 'new'. The Hebrew word occurs only
53 times in the Old Testament, and more than a quarter
of these occurrences fall into the special category of prophetic usage in Jeremiah, Ezekiel and especially Isaiah
40–66.

These prophets are clear that what they expect from
God in the future is qualitatively new, wholly unprecedented. So, Jeremiah foresees a new covenant which
is 'not like' – quite different from – the Sinai covenant
(31:31–32). The new heart and new spirit, which Ezekiel
expects God to give to his people, are as different from
their old counterparts as flesh from stone (11:19; 18:31;
36:26). This sense of what might be called transcendent
newness appears with particular force in the later chapters
of Isaiah which look forward to the unprecedented act of
salvation for his people that God is going to perform. This
will be something unheard of before (48:6–7). It will so
surpass even God's great acts of salvation in Israel's past
that these 'former things' are no longer to be remembered
(43:18–19; 65:17). The remarkable nature of this suggestion should not be missed. Israel's God was a God whose
character was known through his great acts of redemption
in her history. Yet here the prophet says to those whose
faith is 'historical' in this sense, and whose faith for the
future is, understandably, figured on God's faithfulness in
the past, 'Forget the Exodus! This is something really and
truly *new*!' Of course, in reality the prophet himself does
recall the former things (51:9–10; 63:7–16), and he portrays the new as, in some sense, a new Exodus; but the
newness is a vital dimension of this. In the very moment

78

that he uses the analogy he sets it aside as wholly inadequate. Somehow he recognizes that the reality of which he speaks is so new that it cannot adequately be pictured or understood in terms of any familiar images or experiences. This insistence on the radically new in these prophecies of Isaiah 40–66 is surely the reason why Israel did not find their fulfilment exhausted in the eventual return from exile in the sixth and fifth centuries. The language of unprecedented newness in which they are cast overspilt any such historical reality and gave birth to an expectation which we might describe as properly eschatological; that is to say, directed not towards any part of the sequence of events in this world, but to the 'last things' in which this world and its history will be brought to its proper end and thereby transformed into something wholly new.

In these chapters of Isaiah and elsewhere (Isa. 4:5; 41:20; 45:8; 48:7; 65:17–18; Ps. 51:10 [12]; cf. Ex. 34:10) references to the qualitatively new act of God employ the special theological term which is reserved exclusively in the Bible for God's acts of creation (*bara'*). The newness is such as cannot derive from creation itself, since it is new in relation to the creation as such. It derives from the unlimited possibilities of God's creative power. This makes possible even the new creation of the whole of created reality. Hence: 'I am about to create new heavens and a new earth' (Isa. 65:17; cf. 66:22). Or, as the book of Revelation rephrases this divine declaration: 'See I am making all things new' (Rev. 21:5). And the seer explains, also echoing Isaiah, 'the former things have passed away' (Rev. 21:4).

The theological force of this scriptural figure of redemption as a new creation must not be underestimated. What it points to is the claim that, as Christians, our hope is not invested in a repristination of or set of adjustments to the here-and-now, but in a complete overhaul from the foundations up, an overhaul which will result in a decisively

new and different order of existence. While we may properly wish to insist that this 'new' creation will (unlike its
original counterpart) not be *ab initio* (not a *novel* creation)
but precisely a re-creation of the present fallen order,
nonetheless it is vital to recognize that such identity and
continuity as may ultimately prove to exist between the two
will be set within the context of such a radical newness.
Another way of saying this is to suggest that the relationship between the old and the new will be one marked by
a considerable degree of discontinuity. This being so, our
expectations of this new order should not in any way be
constrained or circumscribed by the capacities and inca-
pacities of the world as we know and experience it, but
only by the capacities of the God with whom 'all things
are possible'. This world, in Jürgen Moltmann's careful
phrase, 'cannot bear' the new creation, cannot give birth
to it.[4] The potential for or capacity to produce the new
does not lie latent within the old, but relies utterly on a
new work of the God of the resurrection. The present is
not pregnant with future except insofar as the God of the
virgin conception is at work in its midst calling forth life
where there is only the potential for death and decay.
There may be genuine anticipations of the new order
irrupting in the midst of history. This is how the gospel
writers seem to think about the miracles and signs which
characterized Jesus' ministry. But these are perceived as
striking and surprising as and when they occur precisely
because they do not belong to or fit with our everyday
expectations and perceptions of continuity and order in
the world: they are called forth by fresh initiatives of God's
Spirit at work in the midst of and in spite of the limitations
of the here-and-now.

(HOW) CAN WE SAY WHAT WE DO NOT KNOW?

This discontinuity between the actuality and inherent possibilities of this world on the one hand and the reality of the new creation on the other is accompanied by and necessitates a further discontinuity at the level of our ways of speaking and thinking. When we speak of the new creation we do so using language, appealing to pictures and states of affairs, drawn from this old order, the world as we know and are used to talking about it. The reason for this is straightforward enough: we don't actually have any other language to use! This world is all we know, and all the language we possess is designed to speak of (or on the basis of) what we know of this same world. To introduce the category of revelation at this point does not actually solve this problem but precisely sharpens it. The event of revelation can only reveal something to us if it reaches us where we are, and engages (and in the process no doubt transforms) our familiar ways of thinking and speaking. But there would seem to be a significant problem when the reality revealed is one which itself transcends the proper range of competence within which human speech and thought function. Christian theology has long since known and admitted this to be the case where our knowledge and speech about God himself is concerned. God is not part of this world to which our language belongs and of which alone it is properly fitted to speak; how, then, can there be meaningful talk about this God? The suggestion we are making here is that a similarity exists between this circumstance and that which faces us in speaking about an eschatological future which also (albeit in a quite distinct sense) transcends the range of our mundane speech. Strictly speaking, language belonging to the here-and-now is not fitted to speak of anything more than the here-and-now. But of God and his promised

81

future, speak we must unless we would be content with agnostic silence.

Such silence or agnosticism about God's future cannot be a serious option for Christian faith. The insistence that eschatological statements can and do finally tell us nothing about the shape of the future is therefore just as unhelpful as the suggestion that talk about God itself is incapable of saying anything about him. Why? Because, as we have already suggested, Christianity is a faith which is essentially forward looking and forward moving, orientated towards and living now ever in the light cast backwards by God's promised future. Christian faith, that is to say, is fundamentally a hopeful relation to God and God's world. It transcends the limits of any and every particular human present, looking beyond the often dark and unbearable experiences of the here and now, refusing to accept the suffering, injustice, lack and loss which characterize so much of life, and reaching not upwards to a 'spiritual' escape hatch from this world, but forwards to a time when such things will cease, and the pain and loss be redeemed and refashioned into something good and enduring. Faith is certainly not characterized, therefore, by an attitude of indifference or passivity towards the way the world is. On the contrary, to the extent that it is properly *Christian* faith – faith rooted in the faithfulness of God to his ancient messianic promises and purposes – it will be shaped from first to last by the call to be 'be holy', to be different, to be *in* the world but not *of* the world: and this same call is fulfilled not by turning inwards to form some 'spiritual' community, but by immersing ourselves actively in the very midst of the world's darkest and most depraved corners as salt and light with potentially transforming impact. Faith is a way of being in the world which refuses to submit to the lordship of the here and now, which recognizes a different set of values and goals. Faith sees a quite different purpose and end for this world than that which the world itself presents and points to. It appears as an oddity in history's midst, therefore, seemingly unable to be accounted for, and apparently singing from a different hymn sheet from the rest of humankind. A better image to use might be 'part of a different story', for that is in effect what faith discovers itself to be. The wellspring for a distinctively Christian way of being in the world is to be identified in things which faith believes about the shape of God's future. Christians live, we might say, as characters in a different story, or at least a version of the same story with a radically different ending, an ending which trans-figures the significance of the present in all its dimensions. What is can only finally be understood in the light of what will be; and thus God's future reaches back into the present and bathes it in a quite distinctive light, transfiguring it and generating alternative ways of being in it. To the extent that Christians are at all 'holy', set apart, different from others, this will be due in large measure to the apparent oddity of the fact that they are looking and moving towards an alternative ending to the human story. To be a Christian, a person of faith, we might suggest is precisely to live as a person for whom God's future shapes the present. This being so, it should be clear that agnosticism with respect to the final destiny of the world in God's future is a non-Christian option. The approach to escha-tology which seeks to interpret all statements about this future as veiled or indirect ways of speaking about some-thing else will therefore not bear the weight of responsibility placed upon hope within the logical struc-ture of Christian faith. Bultmann was correct enough to insist that eschatological statements have a vital this-worldly reference and significance (a point to which we shall return in our final chapter), but he misunderstood their logic. Eschatological language bathes the present in the light, not of an abstract 'eternity', but of an identifiable future which lies in God's hands, and which is able to be *and must be* imagined as a catalyst and a pattern for Christian living in the here-and-now. Bultmann's de-mythologizing 'agnosticism' about the future threatens to stop faith dead in its tracks, inculcating an inertia which would imprison faith in a total and despairing present. This would, literally, produce a hope-less theology which would leave Christians more to be pitied than anyone.

We appear, then, to have arrived at an impasse. Talk about God's future is not only desirable but necessary in order for Christian faith to be *Christian* faith at all. It is through speaking in hope, evoking powerful images of a wholly other and transfigured cosmos, that faith is liberated from the patterns of sin and death and thereby contributes directly to the transfiguration of the present. Christian faith moves forward towards the realization of God's kingdom in the slipstream of the statements it makes about that kingdom, the new creation of God. Yet the very substance of Christian faith itself, its forthright appeal beyond the natural reaches of our language and thought forms to a creation which is wholly 'new', forces the admission that such talk is, in the strictest sense, impossible. For of the wholly new we cannot speak. Where, then, does this leave us?

THE LOGIC OF IMAGINATION

It drives us back to a recognition of the essentially imaginative nature of hope and suggests that eschatological statements are, therefore, to be understood above all as imaginative products. Lest this be misunderstood it is probably a good idea at once to introduce a crude but workable distinction between the imaginary and the imaginative. We are not suggesting that Christian hope is imaginary in the sense of being a mere product of human imagining with little purchase or bearing on reality (in this case the reality of the future). Imagination is a much more pervasive and complicated phenomenon in human life than we often recognize, and its products are far from limited to the illusory and the unashamedly frivolous.

One basic function of imagination, as we suggested in Chapter 3, is to enable us to transcend the limits of the given in one way or another. By imagining we are able to make present states of affairs which are otherwise absent, not given in what we are currently experiencing of the world. So, for example, in memory we can often call to mind what has been, presenting – or re-presenting – to consciousness (often with a considerable emotional charge attached) states of affairs, people, places or objects which were once but are so no longer except in our re-membering of them. In prediction or expectation, on the other hand, we reach forward beyond the present in a different direction and envisage how things may be in the future. In neither case are we dealing in any straight-forward manner with 'facts' of experience: Our memories of what has been are always incomplete and often carefully edited to produce a particular 'spin', rose-tinted or other-wise. Our imagining of the proximate future, meanwhile, can only ever be the imagining of one among several possible futures and, as such, may turn out to be either reasonably accurate or quite false. But in both these cases (and many more which we might mention were space to permit it) we recognize that the imagined product is any-thing but a matter of illusion or wanton daydreaming. Imagination, then, is a vital capacity in our attempts to deal with the sphere of the real and the possible.

A third function of imagination is as a source of counter-factuality with respect to or contra-diction of the given. We can always imagine things being other than they are or, perhaps, as they seem to be or we experience them as being. This capacity is, to be sure, the source of illusion and falsehoods. But it is also the source of our ability as humans to protest in the face of the given, to refuse to accept its limitations and lacks and unacceptable features, to reject the inevitability of the intolerable. Furthermore, the capacity to imagine otherwise is basic to our ability to deconstruct the dominant, ideologically generated accounts of who and how and what we are, and to insist on an alternative way of seeing things in our present. Meaning and significance are rendered as we locate particular objects, events and experiences within wider networks of relationships which are not given in experience itself. The quest for meaning, therefore, is always an imaginative exercise in which we locate particulars within such wider patterns. 'Imagining otherwise' is precisely a matter of exchanging one such imaginative framework for another, and thereby seeing the present itself quite differently. The present is transfigured by being configured differently. And configuration is a distinctly imaginative activity of the mind.

A brief concrete example may serve to draw some of these rather abstract sounding threads together, and to refocus our minds on eschatological themes. Christians will wish to construe the world in which we live as one issuing from God's creative love and goodness, as one in which Christ is Lord, and as one invested with a purpose as yet beyond its purview in God's promised future. They will not wish to endorse an account (presented in much popular atheistic apologetics) in which humans are understood as part of a meaningless, complex bio-chemical accident on the surface of a cooling cinder, destined only for eventual atrophy and annihilation. Which of these versions of things we accept will certainly shape the ways in which we experience and act in the present. Neither is given as such within our experience. Each represents a pattern or story conjured up by an imaginative act in terms of which particular bits of experience ('facts') are interpreted and from which meaning is subsequently quarried. An approach to the question of whether one of these accounts is 'true' and the other 'false' is hardly prejudiced by such an account. What we are describing is simply the conditions and capacities pertaining to our experiencing, knowing and making sense of the present. The basic point is that meaningful experience of any sort has a fundamental activity of imagination tangled up with it from first to last.

In the case of our imaginative reconstructions of the past we generally deem ourselves successful to the extent that we are able to reproduce patterns of events, objects and associated circumstances which render for us the original texture of that past. Some of this may be achieved through the activity of personal or social memory (which may, of course, be more or less accurate) and some will have to be built up through inferences drawn on the basis of analogies with our own present experience, stopping the gaps in our knowledge with what we suppose is likely to have been the case. Our imagining of the future, as we have already seen, operates with similar principles. In these instances then, imagination operates in a carefully regulated manner, moving within certain given limits and in accordance with known patterns. It does not invent in any random or capricious manner, but extends the conditions and range of possibilities of the present moment backwards and forwards in accordance with a body of known evidence. The basis on which it does so is the presumption of a substantial degree of continuity between what has been, what is, and what will be, the belief that where human beings and the world in which they live are concerned, certain things can usually be taken for granted.

This belief (and the correctness of it) lies at the heart of the human capacity to understand otherness, to attend to and make sense of people, texts, objects and events which belong somewhere other than within our own familiar world. It is also basic to the power of literature, art and other imaginative products to capture our attention and transform our vision. Making contact with what is shared, they then modify and reconfigure it in surprising ways which help us to see things differently. Usually, though, they do so within unspoken yet agreed limits, leaving the fundamental patterns of reality unchallenged. They present us with a coherent world which is basically identifiable as the world in which we live, albeit now overlaid with otherness.

We have argued that the problem which eschatological hope presents is that of an other-worldliness which posits a ditch, a discontinuity, a break between the fundamental patterns of reality as we know it and the shape of God's promised future in which all things will be 'made new'. In some sense the new creation, while constituting a renewal of the old, will be incommensurable with the old at the most basic of levels. If this is correct then, clearly, the imagination will have to function differently in order to equip our attempts to speak of or to picture it. To help us grasp some of the ways in which it does so we suggest an analogy between the logic of eschatology and those particular products of the imagination which we call fantasy. This is only an analogy. No suggestion is being made that the eschatology *belongs* to the genre of the fantastic. On the contrary, as we shall see, there are some significant differences between the two. We simply draw attention to what may, nonetheless, be some illuminating parallels.

THE NATURE OF THE FANTASTIC

Defining the literary genre or mode of fantasy is a complex business,[5] but for our purposes it is most simply and quickly achieved by pointing to fantasy's most apparent characteristic; namely, its wanton transgression of the rules which, in our familiar world, define the boundaries of the permissible and the possible. 'The actual world is constantly present in fantasy, by negation. . . . fantasy is what could not have happened; i.e. what cannot happen, what cannot exist.'[6] Or again: 'A fantasy is a story based on and controlled by an overt violation of what is generally accepted as possibility; it is the narrative result of transforming the condition contrary to fact into "fact" itself.'[7] In stark contrast to 'realist' literature, fantasy, we might say, deliberately breaches the principle of analogy to which we have already alluded. It posits states of affairs and combinations of events and outcomes which, on the basis of the cumulative fund of shared human experience of the world, are most naturally judged not just unlikely or improbable, but outrageous, non-sensical, impossible. 'The fantastic is always a break in the acknowledged order, an irruption of the inadmissible within the changeless everyday legality.'[8] The things which happen in fantasy, in other words, are things which we are sure do not and cannot happen in the real world.

This transgressive dimension of the fantastic does not limit itself, though, to the positing of occasional sensational happenings in remote corners of an otherwise orderly and familiar world, happenings which, like those chronicled on particular pages of some Sunday newspapers, might titillate or scandalize, but leave the reader's view of reality largely unscathed. The breaches of order which fantasy posits do, of course, manifest themselves in particular 'odd' events; but these are events which, if they are taken seriously, point to far more fundamental and pervasive breaches of the 'natural' order. They are things which, if they happen, must turn our view of the nature of reality upside down and inside out. Or, rather, which dismantle it and leave us unable to put it back together in any meaningful way. Even the most basic categories which shape and render our experience of the world meaningful are threatened with dissolution. Distinctions between past, present and future, self and other, presence and absence, life and death, are all put at risk. 'Fantasy establishes, or dis-covers, an absence of separating distinctions, violating a "normal" or commonsense perspective which represents reality as constituted by discrete but connected units. . . . It subverts dominant philosophical assumptions which uphold as "reality" a coherent, single-viewed entity.'⁹ And what is true at the level of these fundamental physical categories is equally true of moral, aesthetic and political conventions. At every level of human life, the relatively fixed points in relation to which we act and around which we thereby structure our lives are rendered infinitely flexible and inherently unreliable. The very nature of reality, which we all take so much for granted so much of the time, is called radically into question.

Fantasy, then, is clearly parasitic upon given perceptions of what constitutes the real world. It does not attempt to imagine alternative worlds which wholly transcend this one. 'The "creative" imagination, indeed, is quite incapable of *inventing* anything; it can only combine components that are strange to one another.'¹⁰ The fantasist can only begin with what she has by way of raw materials; namely, the world as we know it. Thus 'The fantastic cannot exist independently of that "real" world which it seems to find so frustratingly finite.'¹¹ The distinguishing feature of fantasy, as we have seen, is the way in which these mundane materials are then modified; namely, in ways which deliberately flout conventions and seek to subvert ascendant construals of the real and the possible by disrupting their neat patterns. In fantasy the 'unreal' is deliberately introduced into the midst of the 'real', thereby transforming this world into something strange and unfamiliar. Todorov points us here to a significant distinction within the genre of the fantastic between the respective imaginative products of 'fantasy' proper and what he prefers to call 'the marvellous'.[12] This is a distinction worth taking note of, since, as we shall see, eschatological imagining bears some comparison with both these types.

Characteristic of the marvellous, Todorov suggests, is the generation of an entire alternative imaginative world, coherent in its own right, with its own new set of laws of 'nature', and thus sufficiently clearly other than this world to lift us out of this world and locate us elsewhere. Thus, the achievement of marvel is to construct an alternative, 'super-natural', environment for our imaginative indwelling. Jackson develops this, suggesting that the 'transcendental' world created in marvel is one in which the deficiencies of reality are made good, and in which everything finally makes some sort of sense. It represents a means of imaginative escape from this world into a superior secondary world. The reader is thus reassured and granted some sort of compensatory resolution (albeit temporary) for the perceived absence and loss of life which is his lot in the real. Thus, Jackson observes, 'The world of fairy story, romance, magic, supernaturalism is one belonging to marvellous narrative. Tales by the Grimm brothers, Hans Anderson, Andrew Lang and Tolkein all belong to this mode. . . . The marvellous is characterized by a minimal functional narrative, whose narrator is omniscient and has absolute authority. It is a form which discourages reader participation, representing events which are in the long distant past, contained and fixed by

91

a long temporal perspective and carrying the implication that their effects have long ceased to disturb. Hence the formulaic ending too, "and then they lived happily ever after", or a variant on this.'[13] By its imaginative relocation of the reader in a world clearly other than this one, marvel functions to reassure, and to satisfy the reader's (subconscious or conscious) desire for closure and resolution. It leaves this world largely undisturbed and unscathed except by comparison.

In stark contrast to this, fantasy does not attempt to create anything. It contents itself with a task of disruption. In Jackson's terse description, fantasy 'takes the real and breaks it'.[14] Its basic trope is oxymoron, the juxtaposition of contradictory elements in a unity which makes no progress towards synthesis. It achieves this by introducing into the midst of what is identifiable as this world elements which do not belong, which seem to issue from some other world where other definitions of credibility, possibility, acceptability pertain. Their very presence violates our view of the real, and serves to force reconsideration of it. Hence, Todorov argues, the distinctive mood induced by fantasy is not one of satisfaction at having been lifted out of the mire, but one of anxiety at the disruption of the familiar, and hesitation with respect to the location of the real and the true:

> In a world which is indeed our world, the one we know ... there occurs an event which cannot be explained by the laws of this same familiar world. The person who experiences the event must opt for one of two possible solutions: either he is the victim of an illusion of the senses, of a product of the imagination – and the laws of the world then remain what they are; or else the event has indeed taken place, it is an integral part of reality – but then this reality is controlled by laws unknown to us.[15]

A good example of this literary mode[16] is to be found in Charles Williams' novel *The Place of the Lion*.[17] The book concerns strange happenings in an otherwise sedate 1920s English countryside. A surge of spiritual interest and activity results in Platonic Forms irrupting into the midst of this pastoral world. They do so in the particular guise of exotic animals; a lion, a snake, a huge butterfly, and so on. Each animal represents some character trait, and each exercises powerful influence on those locals in whose personalities these same traits are dominant. Gradually the Powers which govern the structure of creation itself, the eternal Ideas, begin to absorb this fleeting and transient world into their own absolute reality, destroying it in the process. At first the effects are sporadic and scarcely noticeable. They crop up as inexplicable phenomena here and there. Even for those who experience them at first hand, the encounter is one which raises deep questions and leaves uncertainty in its wake about exactly what can have happened. The following brief exchange captures the mood precisely. Two main characters, Quentin Sabot and Anthony Durrant, have had a close encounter with one of the Powers, manifest as a huge lion. Their perplexity is increased by the fact that, on the day of this encounter, a lioness is known to have escaped from a local zoo; but, deep down, they each know that it was no semi-domesticated lioness which confronted them. ' "What do you think? Don't you think it was a lioness?" Quentin cried. And "No," Anthony said obstinately, "I think it was a lion. I also think," he added with some haste, "I must have been wrong, because it couldn't have been. So there we are." '[18]

It is just this evocation of uncertainty and hesitation with respect to the boundaries of the real, frequently (but not necessarily) accompanied by fear born of an encounter with the awe-ful or the unknown, which Todorov sees as essential to fantasy. Once it is resolved, once meaning is

93

found and sense made of the disruption of pattern, we have moved on from fantasy to some other genre, either the 'uncanny' (the recognition that the contradictions are due to the illusory nature of the vision – 'it's only a dream') or the marvellous (the recognition that the vision is not of our world at all but some other alternative world). In either case, our view of the real as such remains more or less intact. It is for this precise reason that fantasy seeks to perpetuate the essential ambiguity of the vision which it presents, not fulfilling or resolving the desire for otherness and transcendence, but heightening it and feeding it by resisting closure, moving ever towards non-conceptuality and indefiniteness, vacillating in its portrayal between the familiar and the impossible, between a vision which both is and yet clearly is not of this world. Significantly, it is not simply the characters in the story who experience this dislocation and disorientation, but the reader also, lacking the comfort of an omnipotent narrator to set his or her mind at rest, struggles to make sense of broken patterns and a narrative mercurial in its refusal to be matched neatly alongside or held accountable by any familiar index of the real. We, too, know what we have seen; and yet we know that we cannot have seen it, because such things do not fit the familiar world otherwise evoked in the text.

This brings us, finally, to consider the purpose behind what may otherwise appear as frivolous and wanton acts of imaginative vandalism with respect to the real. Jackson locates the main driving force behind the fantastic in a fundamental desire for otherness, for transformation, for transcendence, a desire rooted in a perception of absence or lack in the real, and one which will never be entirely satisfied by the construction of 'supernatural' versions of this world precisely because it perceives the need for something more radical, more fundamentally other than any mere rejuvenation or make-over. In its violation of the rules, and its sustained juxtaposition of incompatible elements, fantasy reaches beyond the givenness of this world and expresses a felt need for something so different as not to belong here at all. But such may not be spoken of in any straightforward manner. Thus the fantasist is driven to take the verbal, conceptual and pictorial depictions made available by this world and to fashion from them not a supercharged vision of that same world, but a 'rhetoric of the unsayable'[19] which points precisely to 'an apprehension of something unnameable . . . which can have no adequate articulation except through suggestion and implication'.[20] In the same moment this rhetoric both says and does not say, describes yet does not attempt to describe. It tells us at least that what is hoped for is not containable within the categories of the familiar, but to the unfamiliar itself it can only point obliquely by way of exaggerations, denials and disruptions of the known.

HOPE AND FANTASY

If we turn now to some of the ways in which Christian eschatology is manifest in the text of the Bible we find that its imaginative evocation of God's future bears certain similarities both to 'marvel' and to some of the distinctive features of 'fantasy' as we have described it. These similarities are rooted primarily in the fact that eschatological hope is precisely a bid for otherness and transcendence. Sometimes this bid is expressed through the careful construction of imaginative scenarios which build directly upon both the best and the worst features of this world, exaggerating its contours and furnishing worlds which we can inhabit and even explore in order to satisfy our desire for resolution and fulfilment. To the extent that eschatological imagination functions in this way it draws attention to the assumed levels of continuity between this world and the world to come, and approximates to Todorov's category of the marvellous. At other times, though, eschatological imagination functions differently, bringing this familiar world into imaginative relation with another which, precisely because it is 'new', does not properly belong within it and disrupts it. In such cases the result is closer to 'fantasy' in Todorov's more precise sense. If, following Jackson, we think in terms of two modes rather than discrete genres, it is easier to make sense of the fact that, in eschatological literature, aspects of these two imaginative patterns often coexist within the same text or even the same passage as the writer grapples with and seeks to express the awkward recognition that God's promised future both is and is not like the present, is both continuous and discontinuous with it; such is the radical nature of its essential newness.

We may take as our first example the Old Testament passage which announces the eschatologically new in the most transcendent terms: 'I am about to create new heavens and a new earth; the former things shall not be remembered or come to mind' (Isa. 65:17). The terms in which this passage continues may initially disappoint us. The prophet apparently speaks only of Jerusalem. Its inhabitants live in much the same way as they did in the Old Testament period: they build houses, plant vineyards, keep sheep and oxen, bear children, and die. Virtually all that is different in this vision is that the obvious threats to this kind of life have been removed: they live in peace and security, they enjoy the fruits of their labours, their domestic animals are safe from the attacks of wild animals, no one dies prematurely, and they can expect a secure future for their children. In part we can see how the description is fitted to meet the mundane hopes and desires of a people whose actual negative experiences in life were especially those of living in a land invaded and occupied by enemy powers. Thus far the passage hardly bursts the bounds of historical experience, since even living far in excess of a hundred years would surely recall the patriarchs of Israel's primal history. Or, rather, what does burst the bounds of historical experience here is the prevalence without interruption or exception of what people had enjoyed only in a partial and threatened way. While all this may well be remarkable and improbable, it is not the sort of thing which constitutes a clear disruption of the familiar world, or of which the average hearer or reader is likely to respond with a spontaneous judgement of 'impossible!' In actual fact it is not so different from the kind of utopia many modern historical optimists in the heyday of the idea of progress, whether liberal progressivists or Marxists, have envisaged human history attaining. What the prophet does in this passage, then, is to evoke a vision of God's future which is rooted thoroughly in Israel's familiar world, but which modifies it substantially by replacing lack with plenty, chaos with order, and conflict with peace. The negative features of Israel's experience are imaginatively smoothed away, but the resultant description errs on the side of familiarity rather than unfamiliarity, continuity rather than discontinuity. Even though this is clearly not the 'this world' of Israelite experience, and offers a welcome alternative to their world, it is nonetheless a coherent 'supernaturalized' version of this world, and functions by extending its good points and purging its evils.

The farthest point towards a genuinely transcendent vision of newness is reached in verse 25 where the border between the unlikely and the incredible is transgressed, and an entire alternative ecology substituted for that 'red in tooth and claw' with which the agricultural Hebrews were thoroughly familiar. Were such phenomena as vegetarian lions and wolves which befriend rather than devour lambs to present themselves with any regularity in our everyday experience we should be more than a little surprised, and would be driven to reconsider the basic zoology and biology which we learned in school. It is here alone, then, that the extravagant announcement of a new creation in verse 17 finds any apparent warrant or continuation. Yet it is clear that, if we take it as a literary unity,[21] the prophet expects us to read the whole passage as an account of what will follow the fashioning of new heavens and a new earth. This is not, in other words, a political vision of Israel's historical future, but a genuinely eschatological hope.

If we turn to the New Testament book of Revelation (21:1–5) we find clear allusions to this passage from Isaiah 65, but they are handled in a manner which renders their transcendent reference explicit and in doing so contradicts the original version. So in Revelation 21:4 the voice from heaven declares, 'Death will be no more'. In fact, what Revelation has done is to combine allusions to our passage (65:17–19 to be specific) with allusions to Isaiah 25:7–8, which does speak of the abolition of death. Indeed it is the only Old Testament passage to do this (although Isa. 26:19 and Dan. 12:2 would seem to imply it). Our passage in Isaiah 65 presupposes the usual ancient Israelite view of death, for which *premature* death was certainly an evil, but death at the end of a long and fulfilled life ('full of days') was not. Isaiah 25, like the whole of the New Testament, perceives death itself as an evil ('the shroud that is cast over all the earth') which God can therefore be expected to destroy when he replaces this creation (which is indelibly marked by transience, death and dissolution) with his new creation. Revelation 21 goes beyond the more limited hope of Isaiah 65, and adopts the more transcendent perspective on death of Isaiah 25.

We should observe also that this difference between Isaiah 65 and Revelation 21 in their treatments of death extends to a wider difference. What Isaiah 65 does, as we have already suggested, is to paint a concrete and easily imagined picture of people living in the new Jerusalem, farming their land, bearing children, and so on. Because they are very long-lived, but not immortal, this idyllicized version of historical life in ancient Israel is possible. But eternal life, life in the new creation of God in which death itself has been defeated and abolished, life in which there will be no more marriage or procreation, must be too different from ordinary historical life in ancient Israel for such a straightforward depiction to be possible. Revelation does not attempt it. Instead, it imagines eternal life primarily in negatives ('death will be no more; mourning and crying and pain will be no more'), in pictures which plainly demand to be read symbolically (drinking the water of life, eating the fruit of the tree of life) and in depictions of the physical dimensions and qualities of the heavenly city itself which make it difficult to picture.

Eschatological imagination thus functions rather differently in these two examples. Isaiah 65 offers a concrete utopia which we can imaginatively inhabit. We can harvest the grapes, play with the children, chat to our two-hundred-year-old neighbours, put down straw for the oxen to eat and enjoy watching the lions eat with them. Only with respect to this final image might we begin to find our imagination stretched in such a way as to force upon us the anxious suspicion that, while this appears to be the world we know and are at home in, it just might not be. In Revelation 21, meanwhile, the weight of questioning is much stronger and pushes in the opposite direction: can this strange world really be identical in any sense with the world which we know? The images in which it is depicted are scarcely habitable. It provides no coherent pattern in terms of which we might make sense of its various contents. The sense of dislocation is thus far more acute. The vision draws us out of our present world in the direction of another, and makes us aware in the process that it points beyond itself to something which is, strictly speaking, unimaginable.

We must not misunderstand the nature of this differ-ence. It does not mean that the account in Isaiah 65 should be read as a *literal* description, as if this is exactly what the new creation will be like. This is the mistake which some commentators make when they find the introductory refer-ence to new heavens and a new earth difficult to connect with what follows. The description is not literal but imagin-ative. It is fictive, but intends to be taken seriously as an imaginative account of how things will be in the eschaton. When we reach the concluding 'Thus says the Lord', we should be thinking *neither* 'that's literally what it will be like' *nor* 'this is just an imaginary world which tells us nothing true at all'. The appropriate response is: yes, all that, and, *of course*, unimaginably more and better. The new creation will fulfil the authentic utopias of every gener-ation, and still more and still better. Its transcendence is of an inclusive rather than an exclusive sort. The prophets' visions of it employ both positive (although, of course, inadequate) representations of it, providing fictions which we can inhabit even though they occasionally disturb us by presenting the unfamiliar and the surprising, and more disjointed and bewildering visions whose negations and symbols strain our imagination to the limits, leading us to the very brink of the unimaginable, peering into the bril-liant darkness beyond.

One feature of the gospel traditions in particular illus-trates further and more pointedly the analogy between eschatology and fantasy. The Gospels are, of course, thoroughly eschatological documents designed to direct the reader to the promise of God and its irruption within history's midst in the person and work of Jesus and the Holy Spirit. They tell the story of the relationship between two worlds, worlds which are certainly related as present and future, but which overlap and intermingle in the story of Jesus. Where this overlap occurs, the results are frequently manifest in identifiable disruptions of the patterns of ordinary experience by the appearance within this world of phenomena which do not fit or belong there.

The narration of the ministry of Jesus is filled with examples of this. Before he is even born the story of this man interrupts the ordinary and involves events which herald the advent of one who, while he is in this world is not 'of' it, at least in the sense that his identity is finally bound up with another, coming world and its conditions. The angelic announcement to Mary that she will conceive and give birth to a son meets with a predictable response which is, in a sense, the appropriate response to much of what follows: 'How can this be, since I have not slept with a man?' (Luke 1:34). Mary both articulates the incommensurability which she perceives between the old order and the new (such things do not happen in reality: women simply do not get pregnant without sexual intercourse or some 'natural' surrogate for it), and receives a clue to the source of the anomaly which will hold good throughout all that follows: 'The Holy Spirit will come upon you, and the power of the Most High will overshadow you' (1:35). When God acts through his Spirit to introduce signs and anticipations of his promised salvation into this world there can only be anomaly and surprise, for the two orders do not fit neatly together. The ordinary is rendered untidy by the occurrence of that which does not belong in its midst; and fear and incredulity are perfectly natural initial responses to all this. How can this be? Surely this is impossible, outrageous, unnatural?

In a sense the virginal conception is a first marker laid down in anticipation of much of what follows in the accounts of Jesus' ministry. Typically modern responses to much of what is narrated in the Gospels recognize this well

101

enough. The stories are full of things which it is difficult for intelligent, scientifically educated people to accept. What such responses frequently miss, however, is that the Gospels themselves show us that those same things were mostly no easier for Jesus' own contemporaries to accept. We may be far more aware of the way the world ordinarily functions in terms of precise scientific description; but we are no better placed in terms of identifying things which fly obviously in the very face of the ordinary. The ancients were just as capable of articulating the question 'How can this be?' as we are, as Mary's question shows. And this question was frequently on people's lips during Jesus' life. From his baptism by John to his arrest by the temple guard Jesus was constantly sought out by the crowds and the religious leaders precisely because his ministry was characterized by the extraordinary and the outrageous. In his presence the accepted patterns of normality were stretched and broken up with abandon. Whether it was by deliberately breaking the Sabbath legislation, accusing the religiously observant of hypocrisy and mixing with 'sinners', or by healing the sick, transforming a packed lunch into a meal for the multitudes, and calming the wind and waves, Jesus was forever disrupting the comfortable conventions and expectations of the day, posing uncomfortable questions about the coherence of the assumed social, religious, moral and natural orders alike. In Jesus the open secret of the presence of God's kingdom skewed the smooth surface of the real, and pointed beyond the hegemony of the present to the eventual triumph of God's promised new order. The responses were frequently similar ones: fear and trembling (e.g. Mark 5:33), astonishment beyond measure (e.g. 7:37), perplexity or incredulity (e.g. John 6:41), and, on the part of some, rejection of the challenge by seeking to destroy him (e.g. Mark 3:6, John 11:45f.).

If the virginal conception marks the beginning of this

disruption of this world by the influence of God's future in its midst, it is with the resurrection of Jesus that the disruption reaches its climax and its decisive point. Here, if anywhere, the question 'How on earth can this be?' is forced from the lips of all those familiar with the ascendant order of sin and death which marks this world. The observation that 'Dead men don't rise', far from serving (as it was intended) to undermine the point of the resurrection narratives actually serves to *make* that point rather neatly. Dead people, generally speaking, remain within death's clutches. Death is the ultimate victor in everyone's life, no matter how many small and temporary victories of healing and the prolongation of life we may achieve, and no matter how high a quality of life we may manage to secure for ourselves in the meanwhile. It is all finally just a delaying of the inevitable. We cannot take any of it with us. Death will get us in the end. That is precisely why the resurrection of Jesus from death, viewed in its context as the power of God manifest in Israel's messiah, is so striking an anomaly and so profound a challenge to the prevailing assumptions. Death, in the New Testament, is not simply an event which ends particular human lives, but a metaphor which stands for the universal tendency to atrophy. All that exists is characterized by transience and the movement toward its own eventual demise. Nothing finally endures. Thus the resurrection of Jesus from death is, more than any other single event or combination of events in his life, a breach of the 'orderliness' of this world which scandalizes and turns our view of the whole of reality upside down. If we admit its reality then it leaves nothing the same. Its reality is one which disrupts the pattern of sin and death.

In the accounts of Jesus' resurrection appearances, therefore, we find the now familiar weaving together of ordinary and extraordinary, that which does and that which does not belong in this world. We are certainly not dealing with some other world, but very much with this one in which the events of Jesus' crucifixion seem finally to have sealed the hegemony of death as a force capable of crushing every hope and aspiration. The disciples are locked away for fear that the forces of violence and death will bear them away in Jesus' wake. Some make their way tentatively to the tomb in order to perform the rituals associated with death. Others are already making their way home from Jerusalem having relegated Jesus and all that he stood for to the past tense: 'we had hoped . . .'. It is into the midst of all this so familiar human experience of loss and grief that the risen Lord breaks, unexpected, and to the astonishment of those whom he encounters. While this is the very news that one might have expected them to want to hear and to believe, the initial reaction to this incongruous breach of the universal experience of death is mostly one of fear and an initial incapacity to believe its truth. Secondhand reports will not do. It is only when people meet the risen Jesus himself that they allow themselves to begin to adjust their expectations and commitments to accommodate what has happened. Even these appearances are far from unambiguous. It is clearly Jesus; yet he both is and is not the Jesus they had been with just a few days earlier. He has the relevant scars on his hands and eats fish, so he is not a ghost. But he equally clearly does not belong to this world any longer: he makes sudden, inexplicable appearances and disappearances, and his appearance is such that even those who knew him best do not at first recognize him. This, then, is no extension of the crucified Jesus' mode of presence in the world, but a transfiguration of Jesus through resurrection such that he no longer fits the spatial and temporal conditions of this world at all. The experience of this enigmatic and bewildering incommensurability must surely have convinced the apostles (including Paul) that the promise of a new heavens and new earth was no mere poetic hyperbole, and lay behind reflections such as the following in the early Christian community: 'So it is with the resurrection of the dead. What is sown is perishable, what is raised is imperishable. It is sown in dishonour, it is raised in glory. It is sown in weakness, it is raised in power. It is sown a physical body, it is raised a spiritual body. . . . When the perishable puts on the imperishable, and the mortal puts on immortality, then shall come to pass the saying that is written: "Death is swallowed up in victory." ' (1 Cor. 15:42–44, 54). The reality of the risen Lord could only be understood in terms of the categories which Jewish eschatology already offered; yet these same categories now radiated with a luminousness which hitherto they had lacked. The reality both confirmed and yet transfigured even the clearest of resurrection hopes.

The triumph of life over death, and the forces of life over the forces of death, rather than vice-versa, is the hallmark of God's promised new creation in Scripture. Salvation is participation in 'life in all its fullness'. And life is the characteristic gift of God's Spirit at work in the world. Thus Paul refers to the resurrection body as a 'spiritual' body, a body which belongs to the economy of the Spirit rather than the 'flesh'. It is part of the new creation, not the old. 'To set the mind on the flesh is death, but to set the mind on the Spirit is life and peace' (Rom. 8:6). The characteristic Pauline distinction between flesh and spirit/Spirit is not just moral but eschatological. To live 'in the Spirit' is to live in accordance with the forces of life and to resist that which leads to death, an orientation which anticipates the new creation even in the midst and under the conditions of the old. Thus, for now, it is a matter of struggling with the prevailing order of things, and breaking the pattern of the present. 'Flesh' cannot inherit the kingdom of God precisely because the age of the Spirit involves the crucifixion and subsequent resurrection of the 'flesh' itself in all its aspects. The old must pass away and be broken down in order that it may be raised up again under the form of the new. In this sense, then, the relationship between the crucified Jesus and the risen Lord constitutes the basic pattern for the wider relationship between the old order and God's new creation; and 'the power of the resurrection' is a suitable way of describing that activity of God's Spirit in the church and the world which issues from the event of Jesus' rising and continues in constant events of divine disruption of this world, in healings, in 'miracles' of various sorts, in deliverance from evil powers, in the gradual subversion of the dominion of darkness and death and its replacement by the forces of light and life.

In this way the power of God's promised future reaches back into the present and decisively reshapes it. Of course, whether we are thinking of the New Testament's depiction of such 'eschatological' phenomena or the continuing experience of them in the ongoing history of God's dealings with the world, we are not, strictly, considering works of eschatological imagination. Although the attempt to tell the story of such things (in the Gospels or elsewhere) is certainly an activity of imagination, it is not an imagining of the 'last things' as such, and it is with these that we are chiefly concerned. Nonetheless, in as much as such things constitute genuine anticipations of God's future in the present, we must recognize their ambiguous status: They belong to this world in so far as they occur within it. On the other hand, they do not properly belong to this world because they constitute a disruption of its continuities and potentialities, and point beyond it to a source or influence in a future whose possibilities and potentialities are quite different. They show us this not by representing or embodying the reality of this future in a direct way, but indirectly, by disrupting and refusing to fit neatly within the patterns of history, pointing beyond themselves in their obdurate inexplicability to a reality which even they cannot adequately manifest in the here-and-now because the here-and-now cannot bear the full weight of God's promised future in which all things will be made radically new, and the former things will not be remembered. As such, though, such phenomena serve as a vital model for Christian attempts to imagine the future, which, they suggest, must refuse to be constrained by the limits of the given, reaching ever beyond the possibilities of the present in striking and even daring ways in order to remind us ever afresh that with the God of creation, virgin conception and resurrection, all things are possible. Eschatological imagination must be ambiguous, must disturb the construals of the real and the possible which we otherwise take for granted; otherwise its critical role with respect to our imagining of the present is left unfulfilled.

To sum up, then, eschatological statements are, due to their deliberate and inherent 'other-worldly' reference, both like and unlike fantasy. They are more like fantasy than anything else in their handling of the basic components of our experience of this world, precisely because what they are trying to show us in language drawn from this world is that our expectations of the new creation must not be constrained by our experience of this world. On the other hand, they are unlike fantasy in their intent to refer beyond this world to another which they actually take seriously as a promised reality, and about which they realize Christian faith must strive and be able to say something meaningful. Meaningfulness is not, however, limited to the category of factual or empirically verifiable statements, and it is clear that eschatological statements achieve their goal, if they do, by some other means than straightforward description or factual reference. They do so by the deliberate and sometimes striking and discomforting development and conjunction of ideas and pictures drawn from this world, but presented now starkly in ways which correspond to no this-worldly experience. They may use hyperbole, amplifying both good and bad aspects of our human lot to the point where they become grotesque and wrench us away from our preoccupation with the mundane and the familiar. Or they may function by cancelling out the negative aspects of the known, offering a vision of a world set free (for example) from death and suffering and all the consequences of these in human life. The moment we try to make sense of the biological, or moral, or physical implications of such visions we quickly run aground. But to do this is to miss the point. What the visionaries and dreamers are pointing us to is precisely a new order of things for which their images serve as appropriate symbols, and in relation to which such calculations are frankly meaningless. Or, again, it is quite common in eschatology to find shocking and apparently non-sensical conjunctions of images and ideas, conjunctions which could never be part of our experience in this world. To follow Augustine in seeking out rare examples which demonstrate that they could be is again almost certainly to miss the point. Zoological anecdotes about wolves and lambs actually lying down together without serious collateral damage occurring, or scientific demonstrations of the non-combustibility of human flesh under certain conditions, all this is just about as remote from the intent of eschatological statement as could be imagined. Indeed it serves to undermine its very point, which is to direct our imaginations beyond the conditions obtaining in this world to a new world which we can only as yet imagine, but our hope for which lies in the faithfulness and capacities of the God of the resurrection.

5
ooooooooooo

Images of Hope

At one moment we are told that we make our heaven in the image of this – all too real – world; and at another that our desire creates, by contrast, a mystical region where all the signs are inverted, in order to escape the bondage of society here below and fly to the freedom of our dream world. But we know quite well that our God is different.

(Henri de Lubac)[1]

If we do not permit ourselves to form images of personal and collective existence after death, then we have no way of testing who we are or of sounding our deepest ideals. It's not that we need to know the details of the world to come – life is short and we will get our data soon enough – but we do need to imagine.

(Carol Zaleski)[2]

The Christian religion . . . uses symbolic language about the End in a very particular manner, for it is not concerned to make much ado about Life after Death in general but it must bring out its quite specific Gospel that Life is in Christ.

(Ulrich Simon)[3]

At the heart of Christian eschatology are a series of major images, given in Scripture and constantly reflected on in the tradition. They depict the closing period of human history, the eschatological event itself (the end of history), and the eternal state. In this chapter we shall consider ten

109

of these major images. There are few precedents for this method of studying Christian eschatology by way of images.[4] Systematic treatments of eschatology usually deal in concepts and arguments, noticing images only to reduce them, all too easily and quickly, to bricks or supports in a non-metaphorical conceptual structure. Our method in this chapter attempts to do justice to the primacy of imagination in eschatological thought. This is not a way of evading the need for conceptual clarity or taking a short cut through the debatable issues. In each case the image will be seen to raise significant theological issues. But discussing these explicitly as issues concerning the significance of the eschatological imagery will prove a fresh and fruitful approach to them.

ANTICHRIST

> The ways of history do not lead directly upwards to the Kingdom of God; they pass by way of the final unveiling of the Antichrist, who conceals himself under the last mask to be stripped away, the mask of what is good and what is Christian.
>
> (Hans Urs von Balthasar)[5]

> He walks, the enchanter, on his sea of glass,
> Poring upon his blue inverted heaven
> Where a false sun revolves from west to east. . . .
> He's the false copy where each feature's wrong,
> Yet so disposed the whole gives a resemblance. . . .
> He is the Lie; one true thought, and he's gone.
>
> (Edwin Muir)[6]

One form which the eschatological imagination takes, both in Scripture and in the Christian tradition, is a narrative of events in the closing years of history. Prominent in such narratives is the Antichrist, the last human opponent of

Christ, a universal ruler whose reign is a time of unprecedented evil and whom Christ will defeat at his parousia. For example, in 2 Thessalonians 2, Paul[7] tells of 'the lawless one' (or 'the sinful one') who will be revealed in the future, setting himself above every divinity, declaring himself to be God, and taking his seat in God's Temple. His coming (significantly called here his 'parousia', like the parousia of the Lord Jesus) is associated with a rebellion or apostasy, meaning that those who have rejected the truth of God will believe the lies of Antichrist, encouraged by deceptive signs and wonders wrought by the power of the devil. Finally, the Lord Jesus at *his* parousia will destroy the Antichrist (2 Thess. 2:3–12).

This Antichrist figure in 2 Thessalonians is plainly a religious figure, claiming worship as the supreme divinity, but he is no less also a political figure. The combination is unsurprising against the background of the pervasively religious politics of the ancient world, in which kings and emperors were frequently worshipped as divine. Jews and Christians were unusual in resisting this divinization of earthly power. Antichrist is the extreme case of political religion: he rules the whole world and claims to be the supreme divinity. As such his rule is the evil antithesis of the kingdom of God, which Jesus Christ comes to establish. In Antichrist's empire human power, aided and abetted by the superhuman forces of evil, absolutizes itself in a sort of counterfeit theocracy. Antichrist is the last and supreme expression of the age-old human desire to be God. The serpent's tempting promise that 'you will be like God' (Gen. 3:5) receives its final, though deceptive fulfilment when Antichrist usurps the place of the only true God in the very temple of that God. He thus commits the ultimate blasphemy, while all humanity, except the elect, commit the ultimate idolatry of accepting his claim to be God.

Paul's portrayal of the Antichrist drew on Jewish expectations of a final human enemy of God and his people, and especially on Daniel's prophecy (11:29–49). There the model for this figure is Antiochus Epiphanes, the Syrian king who in the mid-second century BC defiled the Temple, setting up a pagan idol in it. He persecuted Jews who refused to compromise their loyalty to the God of the Torah, while other Jews apostatized by going along with Antiochus' reforms. From this source especially stemmed the expectation of a self-deifying world emperor who would persecute the faithful while receiving the worship of the rest of humanity.

But Jewish tradition also supplied a second kind of eschatological adversary: the false prophet (modelled on Deut. 13:1–5) who by deceptive teaching and miracles will lead people astray from the worship of the true God into idolatry. It would be easy to insert him into Paul's narrative. He would be the one who performs the deceitful miracles that persuade people of the Antichrist's right to their worship.

In fact, this is just what happens in the book of Revelation, which portrays the eschatological opponents as two great monsters, the sea-beast (Rev. 13:1–8) and the land-beast (13:11–18). The first is a world ruler, who blasphemes God and is worshipped by all except the elect. The second, also called the false prophet (16:13; 19:20), performs deceptive miracles, persuades people to make an image of the sea-beast, and even enforces worship of the sea-beast by coercive measures. Behind the two beasts lurks the supernatural power of evil, represented in Revelation's imagery by the dragon.

In addition to the two beasts, Revelation also adds a third form of human evil in league with them: the harlot who stands for the world metropolis Babylon. The sea-beast represents the sheer brute force of political and military power, whose success seems divine and evokes worship (cf. 13:4). The land-beast represents the deceptive power of religious cult and propaganda in the hands of a state religion. The harlot represents the enticements of economic affluence. Even though this is at the expense of the poor of the empire, it is sufficient to seduce the élite, who benefit from it, to support the imperial rule.

Like Paul, Revelation tells an imaginative story of the reign of Antichrist and its end. Unlike Paul, Revelation clearly relates this story to the power of imperial Rome, its idolatrous and corrupting influence, and the resistance to which Christians are called. The traditional images are crafted and elaborated in a masterly way which is both powerfully imaginative and at the same time a penetrating exposure of the political, economic and religious realities of the Roman world of that time.[8] A different New Testament example of the contemporary appropriation of Antichrist imagery is in the Johannine letters, where the only New Testament instances of the word 'antichrist' itself are to be found (1 John 2:18, 22; 4:3; 2 John 7). Here it is Antichrist as the deceiving prophet who is said to have already come in the form of many antichrists, i.e. purportedly Christian teachers who deny that the human Jesus is the Christ. This Antichrist figure has no reference to the external, political world, only to the danger of apostasy by the people of God.

Most contemporary Christians give little, if any, thought to Antichrist, but for most of Christian history he was a very familiar figure.[9] Often he was a figure of the future who featured in an imaginative narration – elaborated from biblical and other sources – of the final events leading up to the parousia. But this did not usually make him a distant danger. He might well appear in the present and not infrequently did. The biblical sources permitted a rich variety of forms in which Antichrist might be imagined or identified. He might be individual – a single monstrous human usurping God's rule over the world – or collective – a political or ecclesiastical power, a religious institution or movement – or he might be both. He might be an external danger threatening the church or a deceptive influence within the church. He might be openly antichristian or masquerade as Christian.

Thus, to instance only some of the more notable identifications of Antichrist (or Antichrists), at various times he was taken to be the pagan Roman empire, Islam, the Ottoman empire, the emperor Frederick II, pope John XXII, the corrupt papacy or the papal institution itself, Martin Luther, the French Revolution, Peter the Great, Napoleon, Mussolini, Hitler, the Soviet Union, the European Union, and Saddam Hussein. Many of these identifications may strike contemporary readers as either silly or pernicious, though some may still seem rather apt. At its worst the Antichrist tradition promoted the demonization of opponents, which was especially dangerous when – in the days of Christendom or even of modern America – the struggle against Antichrist could be undertaken in all-too-worldly, political and military ways. At its silliest the Antichrist tradition became a kind of futurological game for ingenious exegetes to play.

It is not, however, for these reasons primarily that the image of Antichrist largely disappeared from Christian consciousness in the modern period, surviving only in conservative and fundamentalist forms of Christianity, where the biblical images have continued to be taken seriously and often very literally. The main reason for Antichrist's modern eclipse is undoubtedly that he had no place in the future envisaged by the historical progressivism of the modern West, to which the Christian church in the modern West to a large extent adapted its eschatology. The Antichrist image stands in flat contradiction of every kind of progressivist utopianism. It portrays the common future of all human history, not as paradise at last achieved, but as the tower of Babel finally completed, the globalization of humanity's most evil and idolatrous tendencies. If the millennium is the Christian tradition's utopia, the reign of Antichrist is its dystopia. This (the image is surely telling us) is what history will produce if and when God allows it to follow its unredeemed course to the end. Utopia cannot be the product of history, only of God's redemption of history.

This is surely a perspective which the evils of twentieth-century history and the terrors of the incoming twenty-first century enable us to take with fresh seriousness. Evil is not the growing pains of infantile humanity which we are increasingly putting behind us, nor merely the ignorance which the progress of reason gradually dispels. As human knowledge and power over the world increase, so the potential for evil and disaster develops at least equally with the potential for good.

Particularly relevant to the Antichrist image is the now obvious fact that history does not necessarily bring the progressive advance of truth, but constantly magnifies the means and possibilities of obscuring truth and propagating lies. In a media and IT world of docu-soaps, docu-dramas, virtual reality, and endless possibilities of technological manipulation of what our senses tell us, not only do the possibilities of dissimulation and deception multiply alarmingly, but the very distinction of truth and fiction may seem close to vanishing point.[10] Postmodern relativism and subjectivism gain their plausibility perhaps largely from these technological developments.

In the biblical narratives of Antichrist, the possibility of his arrival makes two demands on Christians. One is prophetic discernment. Antichrist is above all plausible and impressive. He offers what everyone wants: security, peace, prosperity. His reign is a seductive counterfeit of the kingdom of God. His cause is advanced not least by false prophets among the people of God. His strength is in the power of the lie, and against him Christians can deploy no other power than witness to the truth.

This is what should guard against the danger of misusing the Antichrist image as a means of demonizing enemies. The question of Antichrist should arise only in the context of an utterly serious attempt to discern the truth of things. In particular it alerts us to the tendency to idolatry that besets especially the powerful and their interests. The absolutizing of anything merely human requires a masquerading as divine, which only reference to the truly divine, the coming kingdom of God, can adequately expose. Anyone, for example, who considers the global economic market an irresistible force which cannot be questioned makes the mistake of those who worshipped the sea-beast, saying, 'Who is like the beast and who can fight against it?' (Rev. 13:4).

The second demand is martyrdom. At its most authentic the image of Antichrist has always been inseparable from the requirement of suffering resistance, exposing the lie by refusing to embrace it even to the point of death. In the reign of Antichrist truth and martyrdom require each other, just as they did in Gethsemane and at Golgotha. This brings the issue of Antichrist close to the christological heart of Christian faith, as it is in Revelation, where the martyrs who triumph over the beast by refusing his lies are 'those who bear the witness of Jesus', and in 1 John, where the defining test of the prophets of Antichrist is christological. It is only by following Jesus in his witness to the truth of God at all costs that the church can finally show that the Antichrist's sham theocracy is not the kingdom of God. One of the key instances in which the Antichrist narrative has been played out in twentieth-century history is that of the Confessing Church under the

Nazis, for which it was the lordship of Jesus that exposed the antichristian character of the Nazi regime and its false prophets the German Christians.

This suggests, finally, the question: Is the story of Antichrist an imaginative narrative about the final part of human history or an imaginative portrayal of what human history may be like at any time? Perhaps in a sense it has to be both. As an imaginative exposure of what human history would come to were God to let it run its course without restraint (cf. 2 Thess. 2:6–7), it exposes those tendencies of human history – 'the mystery of lawlessness already at work' (2 Thess. 2:7) – which so far have not been allowed to run beyond all restraint. Whether or not they ever will, it is from that ultimate dystopia that the final coming of God's kingdom must redeem human history.

THE PAROUSIA

> Christian eschatology does not speak of the future as such. It sets out from a definite reality in history and announces the future of that reality, its future possibilities and its power over the future. Christian eschatology speaks of Jesus Christ and *his* future.
>
> (Jürgen Moltmann)[11]

> We do not know what is coming, but we know who is coming to us.[12]

The 'coming' (Greek: *parousia*) of Jesus Christ at the end of history (often known in the Christian tradition as 'the Second Coming' or 'Second Advent') is the focal image in New Testament eschatology. All else depends on it. The biblical story of God's redemption and renewal of his creation focuses on Jesus, not only centrally – in his life and death and resurrection – but also finally – in his parousia. Since Jesus is the human person on whom the destiny of the whole world hangs, his story is unfinished until the story of the whole world is complete, and, conversely, the world's story is unfinished until he comes to complete it.[13] The coming of Jesus Christ is the focus of Christian hope because his future is our future and that of all creation. This certainly means more than simply that the future is 'Christ-shaped', a future related only to his past.[14] It means that Jesus *himself*, the incarnate Son of God who in his risen and exalted humanity is still human as well as divine, has a future with the world which is really both his own and the world's future. If the image of the parousia did not tell us something about Jesus himself, it would not tell us anything about the human destiny which Jesus pioneers and models not only now but for all eternity.

The major difficulties of envisaging the parousia are two. One is that it is the event which brings the temporal history of the world to an end. It is not just the last event of world history, but the event that ends history. It cannot be an event in time and space like the other events of history, since it is the event that happens to all time and space and transforms them into eternity. Yet the only kind of event we can imagine is one which happens in time and space. So it is that the New Testament pictures the parousia as an occurrence, with a temporal sequence, in which Jesus descends from heaven to earth. Most often he is pictured as resplendent in heavenly glory, seated on clouds and attended by a vast retinue of angels, arriving on earth like a king entering his kingdom (e.g. Matt. 16:27–28; 1 Thess. 4:16; Jude 14–15).

Recognizing (as we have argued in Chapter 4) that in such biblical descriptions we have not history written in advance, but the work of the eschatological imagination can help us also with the second difficulty in envisaging the parousia. This is the difficulty of envisaging a truly

universal event effected in person by one human individual. The expectation that 'every eye shall see him' (Rev.
1:7) would be difficult to take literally even in the ancient
conception of the world. Today we should have to entertain
the ludicrous image of the returning Jesus as a sort of
space satellite circling the earth in all directions. Some
literalist readings of biblical prophecy suggest in all seriousness that the parousia will be visible to all by appearing
on their television screens. But the recognition that the
parousia transcends history frees us from the need for such
realistic speculations. The relation of Jesus himself to the
ultimate future of all creation can be understood theologi-
cally in terms of his role in the divine purpose as the one
who is uniquely identified both with God and with all
humanity. The New Testament's imaginative portrayals of
this should be taken seriously, not literally.

Much of the imagery used of the parousia in the New
Testament depicts in some way or other the achievement
by Jesus Christ of the full and final sovereignty of God over
the world. He comes as the king to sit on his throne of
judgement (Matt. 25:31–46). He is the judge who already
stands at the gates of the city about to enter (Jas. 5:9). He
comes as the warrior king leading the heavenly armies to
victory over the assembled forces of the world's opposition
to God (Rev. 19:11–21). He comes to deliver those who
are loyal to God's rule from the evils and the enemies that
afflict them while God's rule is contested (2 Thess. 1:9–10;
Heb. 9:28). He comes to judge all people, living and dead
(Acts 10:42; 2 Tim. 4:1; 1 Pet. 4:5). Every creature in the
universe will bend the knee before him and acknowledge
his lordship as that of the only sovereign God (Phil.
2:10–11).

It is notable that behind many such passages lie Old
Testament prophecies of God's 'coming' to perform a
definitive act of salvation or judgement. For the New Testa-

ment writers, Jesus' coming as Saviour and Judge is God's eschatological coming to his creation to establish his kingdom. It is the event in which all that is presently at odds with God's rule over his creation must be judged and destroyed before the creation itself is perfected in the eternal presence of God.

As well as his coming or arrival, the parousia is also described in the New Testament as the revelation (e.g. 1 Cor. 1:7) or appearing (e.g. 1 Tim. 6:14) of Jesus. Both types of language make clear that the parousia is envisaged not merely as the culmination of what is presently happening, but as a divine act of eschatological novelty over against the present state of things. The Jesus who is presently absent from the world will come to it in order to do what he is not now doing. The Jesus who is presently hidden from the world will be made manifest. Of course, the image of Jesus' coming does not imply that he is not in important senses present in the world now. But he is not now present for the purpose for which he will come at the end: to judge.

While the language of coming makes it especially clear that the parousia brings not just more of the same, but something new, the language of hiddenness and manifestation or revelation also makes this point in its own way. What is hidden now is Jesus' heavenly glory, his lordship over the whole world which his sitting on God's heavenly throne at God's right hand portrays, and also his fellowship with his people in which their true nature as his people is hidden.

This present hiddenness of Jesus' rule is what means, for example, that in the book of Revelation the beast's power can appear godlike and invincible, triumphant over the Christians whom he puts to death. The real truth of things from God's perspective – for example, that the martyrs, by their witness to the truth even to the point of death, are the real victors – breaks through to those who have eyes to see, but it is only at the parousia that it finally prevails as the truth which all must acknowledge. This revelation is more than the unveiling of what is already true, because the unveiling itself makes a difference: no longer can anyone pretend or be deceived, those who wield power by deceit can do so no longer, all illusions and delusions must perish before the truth of God and all who insist on clinging to them must perish also. It is in this sense that Jesus, though already seated on the throne of the universe, has not yet brought all things into subjection to God. The revelation of his lordship will also be its final implementation. Since the imagery of kingship, war and judgement can be unpalatable and misleading today, it may be helpful to elucidate its meaning by means of the equally biblical picture of the final revelation of truth and its power to dispel all lies and impostures.

From this point of view, the parousia is the event which concludes history by making the final truth of all things manifest to all. Hence the language of 'revealing' and 'appearing' is used in the biblical texts not only of Jesus, whose true relationship to the world is made evident to all, but also of all that his judgement of every person who has ever lived will bring to light (1 Cor. 4:5). There is nothing hidden that will not be uncovered (Matt. 10:26). The full and final truth of each person's life will be made known, not least to that person. Similarly, the language of 'revealing' and 'appearing' is used of the final destiny of those who believe in Jesus, 'a salvation ready to be revealed in the last time' (1 Pet. 1:5; cf. Col. 3:4). The parousia is that revelation of all that is now hidden, the disclosure of the full and final truth of all who have lived and all that has happened, that determines the form in which this present creation can be taken into eternity.

Thus in the parousia, both as coming and as unveiling,

something happens which, in relation to the world as it is now, will be both new and conclusive. Once again we find ourselves confronted with the inescapably transcendent character of Christian eschatology. The parousia cannot be taken as a symbol merely of the outcome of history that history itself will provide. It is the future which comes to God's creation from God and comes in the person of the one God has already given to the world as its Saviour and Lord.

RESURRECTION

> One short sleepe past, wee wake eternally,
> And death shall be no more; death, thou shalt die.
>
> > (John Donne)[15]

> > In a flash, at a trumpet crash,
> I am all at once what Christ is, since he was what I am,
> > and
> This Jack, joke, poor potsherd, patch, matchwood,
> > immortal diamond,
> > > Is immortal diamond.
> > >
> > > (Gerard Manley Hopkins)[16]

Resurrection is in origin not a concept, but an image. It pictures the dead person, who has been lying in the grave, standing up again – or being raised up again by God (e.g. John 11:24). There are other biblical ways of picturing the reality to which this image points. The dead may be pictured as asleep in the grave until they wake up again (Dan. 12:2). The dead in their tombs, it is said, hear the voice of the Son of God commanding and summoning them to life and come out of the tombs (John 5:25, 28–29). The personified places – the sea or the underworld – which hold the dead, as it were, in safekeeping until God requires them back, are pictured as surrendering back the dead to life (Rev. 20:13). The dead may be imagined as sown in the earth like seed from which new life will one day flower (1 Cor. 15:36–38, 42). Resurrection as a theological concept depends on these images, since only in such pictures drawn from life this side of death can the gift of eternal life to the dead beyond death be envisaged.

Several of these images of resurrection, including at least the first three we have listed above, might in themselves suggest no more than resuscitation – a return to this mortal life. They could describe the miracles of resurrection performed by Jesus (cf. Mark 5:39; Luke 8:14–15; John 11:43–44), which merely restored people recently dead to mortal life again. By contrast, the resurrection of Jesus and the coming resurrection of the dead at the end of history are clearly understood in the New Testament as entry into a wholly new kind of life, beyond the power of death. Resurrection is then not merely restoration but transformation. While only Paul's metaphor of the seed, among the images listed above, makes this explicit, there are other passages in which it is clearly enough portrayed (Dan. 12:3; Matt. 13:43; Mark 12:25; Phil. 3:21).

It is important to notice that the major images of resurrection are all holistic – in the sense of treating the whole human person as an integral whole. They envisage the dead person returning to life, whether the dead person is pictured as the corpse in the grave (most cases) or as the shade in the underworld (Rev. 20:13). They are not images of spiritual survival of death, like the Greek picture of death as the liberation of the spirit from the prison of the body. The point is not whether or not anything survives: most Jews and Christians in the New Testament period thought that something did. But such survival is merely survival in death, the state of the dead. Resurrection is something else: the restoration of the whole bodily person to life. It is more than that – since the life given to the dead surpasses mortal life – but it is not less than that.

The images therefore picture a reversal of death: the sleeping wake, the dead come out of the tombs. Resurrection does not belong to the immanent capacities of created human nature, which end in death. Resurrection is a fresh creative act of God, giving life back to the creatures who would otherwise revert to the nothingness from which his first act of creation brought them. The voice of the Son of God calling the dead to life (John 5:25) is equivalent to the creative word of God which effected creation in the beginning (Gen. 1). It follows that hope for resurrection is not based on analysis of human nature, as Plato's proof of spiritual immortality was and as arguments for the immortality of the soul advanced by some philosophers of religion still are,[17] but rather on faith in God. Resurrection hope is radical faith in the God who remains faithful to his material and mortal creation, valuing it too much to let it perish. Christian resurrection hope is radical faith in the God who became incarnate in material and mortal human nature, setting the seal of his own presence on its eternal value for him. Christian resurrection hope is radical faith in the God who raised Jesus from death, thereby pledging himself to raise also those who believe in Jesus.

The images of holistic resurrection presuppose the Jewish and Christian understanding of the body as integral to human personal identity, by contrast with the Greek philosophical view that the real person is immaterial spirit. At this point it will be helpful to clarify Paul's discussion of the form in which the dead rise (1 Cor. 15:35–49), since this has so often been misunderstood and the misunderstanding perpetuated by misleading translations of the key terms.

While Paul certainly contrasts the bodily forms of mortal and resurrected people, the contrast in verses 44–46 is not between a 'material' body and a body made of spirit or in some way 'immaterial'. A 'spiritual body' in this sense would be a straightforward contradiction in terms. The key terms are *soma psychikon* and *soma pneumatikon*, in which *soma* is 'body' and the two adjectives are formed from the nouns *psyche* and *pneuma*. A *soma psychikon* cannot be a body made of *psyche*. It must be a body animated by *psyche*, which is the natural life of this world, the life that ends in death. The body is qualified by the kind of life it has, not by the substance of which it is composed. Similarly a *soma pneumatikon* must be a body animated by *pneuma*, which is probably the Holy Spirit, the divine, eternal life given to those who are raised from death.[18] Nothing is said about the relative physicality of the two forms of body.

The other contrasts Paul draws between the two forms of body are: perishable and imperishable, lowly and glorious, weak and powerful (vv. 42–43). These indicate a risen body lacking the mortal body's susceptibility to pain, injury, degradation and death. More than that Paul cannot say. What he says scarcely goes beyond what he and other early Christians knew of the mortal and the risen Christ, who indeed – in his bodily identity in death and resurrection – is explicitly Paul's model for our death and resurrection (vv. 47–48). Similarly, the writer of 1 John is content to admit that we do not know what we shall be, only that when Jesus appears, at the parousia, we shall be like him (1 John 3:2).

Some twentieth-century theologians (notably Barth, Pannenberg and Moltmann)[19] have proposed that bodily resurrection be understood as the raising into eternity of precisely the whole temporal life which the dead have lived. In that case, it is unambiguously the same body which is raised. This proposal should be taken, not as an explanation of the biblical images of resurrection, but as another image of resurrection. Like the biblical images, it cannot in itself be adequate, particularly since it is very difficult to understand the resurrection of Jesus as this and no more. But it may be illuminating to think of eternal life not as a temporal line extending forwards from the moment of death, but as a new kind of temporality into which the whole diachronic extent of a person's life is in some way taken through healing and transformation. The person who dies suffering from Alzheimer's disease, for example, will in the resurrection be who she was in the whole of her mortal life, not merely who she finally was at death. That we cannot imagine how this literally could be is, of course, beside the point. We cannot imagine what resurrection as such will literally be. The case made in Chapter 4 for the necessarily imaginative nature of eschatological assertions applies to the particular images which are our only access to the notion of resurrection.

Since the church's struggle with Gnosticism in the second and third centuries, bodily resurrection (though often conceived as the resurrection of the body to be reunited with the immortal soul) has been orthodox belief, a doctrinal bulwark against Manichean or Platonist depreciations of matter, a reminder that the material world, including human bodies, is God's good creation, with eternal, not merely transient, value. The persistent influence of Platonism in the Christian tradition has frequently meant that in practice Christians have believed in the immortality of the soul rather than bodily resurrection. Other influences in the modern period have made this still the case in much popular belief, despite the fact that modern scientific understanding of human nature makes holistic resurrection more easily meaningful for us than disembodied survival.

But bodily resurrection is a decisively important feature of the orthodox hope for a further reason. Not only is the body integral to human personal identity; it is also the medium of human sociality and of human solidarity with the rest of the material creation. Whereas a hope for purely spiritual immortality envisages human destiny as apart from this world and tends to envisage it in individualistic terms, the hope of bodily resurrection cannot stop at either the human individual, without human sociality, or at humans without the rest of God's creation, in which as bodily creatures we are so deeply embedded. Modern scientific insight into the depth and extent of our continuity with the rest of the animal creation merely reinforces what the Christian hope of bodily resurrection already implies, as Paul recognized in Romans 8:19–23. Our destiny is bound up with that of the world, and our resurrection will be our participation in God's new creation of all reality.

NEW CREATION

> Obviously we need to know nothing beyond the fact that even in eternity there will be a world.
>
> (Emil Brunner)[20]

> At our resurrection
>   both heaven and earth will God renew,
> liberating all creatures,
>   granting them paschal joy, along with us.
>
> (Ephrem the Syrian)[21]

The image of new creation is one that has already featured prominently in the argument of our previous chapters. It has done so, both because it is probably the most general and all-encompassing image of eschatological salvation and renewal (though the image of the kingdom of God could also be seen in that way), and also because it clearly entails the transcendent aspect of eschatology, which we have found it important to stress against purely immanent eschatologies, without lapsing into a wholly discontinuous and other-worldly view of the eschatological future.

New creation, by evoking an analogy with creation in the beginning, requires us to think of a newly creative act of God in which possibilities will be realized which do not belong to the immanent potentiality of the first creation as such, but which come from the transcendent potentialities of God's creative power and love. At the same time, new creation is – paradoxical as this may at first sound – the new creation *of this present creation,* its renewal, not its replacement. New creation is precisely that future of the present world, of all created reality, which does not emerge from the history of this world but will be given to it by God. It requires an originating act of God, just as creation in the beginning did, but in this case it will be an act which preserves the identity of the first creation while creatively transforming it. Just as, according to Jesus' saying, we can find ourselves only by losing ourselves, so the world, the whole of created reality, will find itself, its own true identity given back to it and fully realized for the very first time, through losing itself in God. The continuity between this world and its eschatological destiny will be given it by God in and through the discontinuity of God's new creative act.

This Christian hope that the whole of created reality will be renewed by God, glorified by his presence and taken into union with his own eternal life has maintained only a rather tenuous hold on the Christian imagination for much of Christian history. It is perhaps here that the legacy of Platonism in the Christian tradition has had its most extensive effect. The bulwark which the dogmatic affirmation of bodily resurrection has with difficulty maintained against the complete spiritualizing of human destiny has been less effective against the persistent tendency to understand human destiny as a destiny apart from the rest of creation. Human nature has been so abstracted from its continuity and solidarity with the rest of the material creation that its distinctiveness – in rationality and awareness of God – has been misunderstood as its unique fitness for eternity. So the Christian hope has constantly been understood as hope for human fulfilment in another world ('heaven') rather than as hope for the eternal future of this world in which we live.

This other-worldliness has not been as detrimental as has often been alleged. Innumerable Christians whose spirituality and hope were radically other-worldly – for example, many members of the religious orders in the medieval period and subsequently – have devoted their earthly lives to such this-worldly activities as the care of the sick and the needy. The modern domination and abuse of the natural world is not, as often claimed, the result of traditional Christian other-worldliness so much as of modern humanity's assumption of godlike power over the world. Medieval flight from nature was harmless compared with modern interference in nature. Nevertheless, the mildly Platonist other-worldliness of the Christian tradition, along with the anthropocentrism which was also a Greek inheritance of Christian theology, deprived Christianity of the will or the power to resist the modern project of technological subjugation of nature. If God's creation is ultimately only a throw-away world, destined to perish when its purpose as a vale of human soul-making is fulfilled, it may not seem to matter too much what we do with it.

The millenarian tradition, as we shall observe in the next section of this chapter, provided from time to time a more or less influential qualification of Christian other-worldliness. But, broadly speaking, the modern period has witnessed the contrast of traditional Christian other-world-liness, the destiny of the individual in another world beyond death, and a wholly immanent eschatology of evolutionary and historical progress, a secular millenarianism of hope for the race but not the individual. What was largely lost was the hope for a *transcendent* future of *this world.* That this is indeed the biblical and Christian hope has been frequently reaffirmed in recent theology, but has still to capture the imagination of most contemporary Christians.

The hope of new creation is the hope of a future for the whole creation which cannot develop out of that creation's inherent potentialities, but can only be given it by a fresh creative act of the transcendent God. What is envisaged is a unique event, comparable only with the original act of creation. Modern scientific understanding of the universe can therefore neither contradict nor affirm it, as though it should in some way be predictable from our knowledge of what the universe is like. Whatever future the universe might ultimately have as a result of its own potential for development and disintegration, the new creation is not that future. The new creation is the wholly new – eschatologically new – future which God will give his creation, and which could not be expected other than as the transcendent act of the transcendent God.

It is an act in which the creation will be both fulfilled and transformed. Retrospectively it will be possible to see that this was the future for which it was always destined by God, the appropriate completion of its history, but equally this future will entail a radical transformation of the world's mode of existence, which we can understand only as transposition into participation in the life of God. Delivered from both transience and evil (Rom. 8:19–23), the world will reflect the divine presence and glory in a way now unimaginable. The world will be glorified by God's presence and God will be glorified by the reflection of the divine glory in creation.

The question of continuity and discontinuity between

the present creation and the new creation is essentially the same question as the idea of human bodily resurrection raises (note the explicit link made in Rom. 8:19–23). Since the language of new creation can be applied by Paul even to the present condition of the Christian believer, already transformed in anticipation of the resurrection (2 Cor. 5:17), it is clear that the biblical pictures of the destruction of the old creation and the appearance of the new (Isa. 65:17; 2 Pet. 3:7, 10; Rev. 21:1) do not really envisage the replacement of this old creation by another, but stress the radical transformation involved in God's creative renewal of the old creation.

If modern scientific understanding of the universe cannot affect the credibility of the hope of new creation, it can have an effect on the way we understand the new creation. In biblical times the non-human creation was understood largely statically. There was no thought of stars and planets forming over immense periods of time, of continents moving, of species appearing and disappearing, and so on. The sense in which it is now very clear to us that the creation has its own long and eventful history apart from humanity was unknown to ancient people. The biblical writers did not therefore need to consider whether the new creation will happen to creation only as it will be at the instant of its end or to creation as it has been throughout its existence.

But for us to think of God's taking of the whole of creation into his eternal kingdom would seem to mean imagining the new creation as happening not only synchronically to the whole world as it will be at the end but also diachronically to the whole temporal course of creation's history. In other words, we need to move beyond the picture that no doubt many Christian believers unthinkingly adopt, in which it is only to the world as it is at the end of history that the eschatological transformation of things will happen, while the temporal line that runs from our present to the end of history simply then continues on into the eschatological age beyond. This is to give a kind of temporal privilege to the final state that the world will attain within history that resembles the immanent hopes of the modern ideology of progress more than it does the biblical images of eschatology. Rather in a way similar to the image of resurrection as the raising into eternity of the whole diachronic extent of a person's temporal life, which we suggested in our previous section, so the new creation of all things will be a taking, through transformation, into eternity, of all that has ever happened throughout the aeons of this world's time.

Only in this way can we affirm that 'nothing will be lost', that everything of value in God's good creation, all that God himself treasures and will not let disappear into nothingness, will be gathered into the new and eternal creation. Needless to say, it is absurd to suppose we could understand how this unprecedented act can happen. It bounds our knowledge as it does the creation itself.

Such a perspective should affect the way we value creation. It is a throw-away world neither in the sense of other-worldly eschatology nor in the sense of the modern progressivist project which destroys nature in the attempt to recreate it as we wish.

THE MILLENNIUM

Christian eschatology – eschatology, that is, which is messianic, healing and saving – is millenarian eschatology.

(Jürgen Moltmann)[22]

All the things that the poets said happened in the Golden Age when Saturn reigned will then take place.

(Lactantius)[23]

132

For much of Christian history a considerable number of Christians (called millenarians or millennialists or chiliasts) have expected a period of earthly perfection, in which conditions of life in this world will be radically transformed, prior to the end of the history of this world and the new creation. This ideal time is known as the millennium because millenarians have identified it with the period of a thousand years described in Revelation 20. For millenarians this period has a penultimate and transitional character. It is envisaged as a temporal and temporary period of earthly perfection preceding the final and eternal state of heavenly perfection. Of course, for millenarians who expect the imminent arrival of the millennium it is likely to loom much larger in their imagination than the new creation does, but in principle it is only a penultimate goal of God's purpose.

The millennium's special character as an eschatological hope lies in its this-worldly form, and no doubt this also constitutes its special appeal. It represents the expectation that God is going to achieve his kingdom in this world, to eliminate evil from and to bring to perfection the conditions of life – political, social, economic, natural – which belong to this creation. The this-worldly character of the millennium appears the more prominently in contrast to the strong tendency in the Christian tradition to envisage the new creation and the eternal state in very other-worldly terms. The more this looks like a replacement for the present creation, the more appealing it may seem to expect God to perfect this creation before replacing it with another.

Much discussion and controversy about the millennium revolves around the disputed exegesis of Revelation 20.[24] This is natural insofar as this text is the main exegetical peg on which millenarian belief has hung. But it is unfortunate insofar as the millenarian tradition in Christianity has an importance independent of this exegetical issue. Those who are not convinced by the millenarian exegesis of Revelation 20 are mistaken if they suppose that this authorizes them to ignore the Christian millenarian tradition, a tradition which has by no means always been confined to sectarian groups but in some periods has exercised a wide popular appeal and in some periods has been important even in the mainstream theological tradition.[25] A phenomenon of such importance in Christian history deserves more than exegetical attention.

To turn from the millenarian tradition to the text of Revelation 20, in a serious attempt to read the text itself in its context in the book, is to be surprised by how little Revelation says about the millennium. The millennium in fact fulfils one very specific function within the visionary narrative of Revelation.[26] It portrays the vindication of the martyrs which Christ's victory over the earthly powers of evil at his parousia (Rev. 19:11–21) must entail. In the great conflict between the beast and the faithful followers of Jesus, as Revelation has portrayed it, the beast appears to reign victoriously and to wield the absolute power it claims, while the martyrs, those who witness to the rule of God and Christ, appear to be defeated. From the heavenly perspective of John's visions, however, it is the martyrs who are the true victors. When, at the parousia, this heavenly perspective finally prevails on earth, so that the real truth of things becomes evident, not only must the beast be seen to be defeated, but also the martyrs must be seen to triumph. Appearances must be reversed so that appearance now corresponds to truth. While the kings of the earth who had shared the beast's blasphemous rule are deprived of their kingdom, the martyrs now reign with Christ. While the beast suffers the second death and his followers are killed (19:20–21), the martyrs come to life and the second death has no power over them (20:6).

Life and rule – the two issues on which the conflict between the martyrs and the beast had focused – are the sole themes of the account of the millennium (20:4–6). In both cases the concern of the account is to show not only that the reality of the martyrs' rule corresponds to the pretence of the beast's rule, but also that it far surpasses the beast's rule. The life the martyrs now live is eschatological life beyond the reach of death. Their kingdom lasts not the mere three and a half years allowed to the beast, but an unimaginably long period.[27] In order to demonstrate that their triumph is not one that evil can again reverse, the devil is given a last chance to deceive the nations (20:7–8). But this is no rerun of the rule of the beast, who was allowed to put faithful Christians to death and thus to appear to triumph. This time the citadel of the saints proves impregnable (20:9).

The image of the millennial reign, as employed here, portrays the vindication of the martyrs at the parousia. It portrays this by telling a story, but, once we get over the tendency even of scholarly commentators to read the images of Revelation literally wherever possible, there seems no reason why we should take the image as literally predicting a period. If we do not suppose that there is to be a monstrous animal with seven heads and ten horns, why should we suppose that there is to be a period of rule by the saints? The millennium is a symbol of an aspect of the meaning of the parousia – that the martyrs are vindicated as the true victors. It tells a story in order to give imaginative form to this vindication.

Such a non-literal reading of the millennium seems confirmed by two facts. One is that the only information John gives us about the millennium – that the martyrs live and reign with Christ – is also true of the New Jerusalem (22:5). If the millennium is taken as an actual period of time, then Revelation gives it no function in the purpose of God that the New Jerusalem does not also have. (Millenarians, of course, give it other functions, but not Revelation 20.) Secondly, taking the millennium literally raises a whole series of puzzles about it which interpreters have endlessly discussed: Whom do the saints rule? Do they rule from heaven or on earth? How is the eschatological life of resurrection compatible with an unrenewed earth? Who are the nations Satan deceives at the end of the millennium? And so on. The millennium becomes incomprehensible once we take it literally, but is perfectly comprehensible as a symbol of the eschatological vindication of the martyrs.

It is not surprising that in Christian history the millennium has sometimes been especially the hope of the martyrs, as it was in the pre-Constantinian period generally and in the work of Irenaeus in particular. But, from our earliest evidence of Christian millenarianism in the early second century onwards, the millennium has always meant more than the vindication of the martyrs. It has meant the restoration of paradise in the natural world, peace among people and between people and nature, material abundance, the abolition of pain and poverty, social equality, perfectly just government, genuine theocracy, the restoration of Israel to her central place in God's rule of the world, and so on. The details and emphases of the vision have, of course, varied, but in general the millennium has been the focus of Christian utopian hopes of a perfected state of earthly human society and the natural environment.

In this respect the earliest millenarianism was dependent on and continuous with Jewish tradition in some of the Jewish apocalypses, which expected an interim messianic kingdom on earth prior to the new creation. While Revelation 20 makes use of this tradition for one specific purpose only, the Christian millenarian tradition followed it in seeking the fulfilment of the Old Testament's more this-worldly prophecies of salvation in the millennium. Pagan portrayals of the golden age of the past also fed into the Christian millennium, and in general the millenarianism of each place and time has formulated its millennial ideal in ways appropriate to its particular context. Quite often, though by no means always, these have been the hopes of the poor and the oppressed for social justice and an end to the oppressive political and economic systems of this age.

The millenarian tradition must be taken seriously because it has been in many respects the guardian of the more immanent and this-worldly aspects of the Christian eschatological hope.[28] Other aspects of this hope, such as the vision of God and the glorification of all creation in the eternal life of God, are by comparison more transcendent and in a sense other-worldly. In the millenarian tradition these two sides of the Christian hope have been assigned respectively to the millennium and the eternal state. In the non-millenarian Christian tradition, the more immanent and this-worldly side has been neglected, while in the secular millenarianisms of progress in the modern age, the more transcendent and other-worldly side has been left aside completely. Christian eschatology needs both sides of its traditional hope, and it needs the millenarian tradition to remind it of the immanent and this-worldly side. But it does not seem necessary to follow the millenarian tradition in its temporal distinction between the new creation in eternity and a this-worldly kingdom of Christ which precedes it.

What is necessary, as we suggested in the preceding section of this chapter, is to understand the new creation itself not as a replacement for the present world but as the eschatological future of this world. If – but only if – the new creation is understood in this way, then it is an eschatological conception in which the this-worldly and the other-worldly are not incompatible but are the two aspects of the one eschatological reality. The discontinuity between creation here and now and creation renewed and transformed does not cancel the continuity between them. The present creation finds its goal and perfection in its eschatological renewal, the new creation; it does not need a preliminary and provisional goal within history. Since eschatological thought is an imaginative picturing of the unimaginable, we may have to use alternative images to represent different aspects of the eschatological hope, but we can understand these images as different angles on the one eschatological reality. It is not their compatibility when read as literal predictions that matters, but their theological coherence as images which focus different aspects of the meaning of God's promises for the world. The importance of the imaginative function of eschatological language which we expounded in Chapter 4 comes once more into its own here.

The attention the millenarian tradition draws to the this-worldly side of the Christian hope is important in part because it is this side of the eschatological hope which provides motivation for some aspects of Christian life now, both positively as goal and negatively as eschatological proviso. On the one hand, it offers a utopian model to inspire responsible and hopeful activity in this world, aimed at partial and anticipatory approximations to the coming kingdom within the life of this world. (This is the aspect of the eschatological hope which we shall develop more fully in Chapter 6 below.) On the other hand, it also reminds us that neither this world nor the church in this world is yet the eschatological reign of the saints with Christ. The this-worldly side of the Christian hope can empower a theology of Christian resistance to the dominant powers when, as in the Roman empire or the medieval papal monarchy or modern totalitarian states or contemporary economic hegemony, they claim the absoluteness of theocracy and silence all dissent that might call this realized millenarianism into question.[29] Here also the millennium in its strictly biblical role comes into its own: it empowers those who must expose the lies of Antichrist and stand for the truth of God's rule against all earthly appearances.

THE LAST JUDGEMENT

> Almighty Judge, how shall poor wretches brook
> Thy dreadful look,
> Able a heart of iron to appall,
> When thou shalt call
> For ev'ry man's peculiar book?
>
> What others mean to do, I know not well;
> Yet I hear tell,
> That some will turn thee to some leaves therein,
> So void of sin,
> That they in merit shall excel.
>
> But I resolve, when thou shalt call for mine,
> That to decline,
> And thrust a Testament into thy hand;
> Let that be scann'd,
> There thou shalt find my faults are thine.
>
> (George Herbert)[30]

The notion of eschatological judgement is conveyed in Scripture by two main images: judgement by military victory and judgement in a court of law. The latter is what has traditionally been called 'the last judgement', and it is to this that the Creeds refer (Jesus Christ 'will come to judge the living and the dead'). A long tradition of Christian art once depicted it, with Christ the Judge con-

signing the damned to hell and the redeemed to paradise.
It must have been one of the most familiar religious scenes
for medieval Christians. However, in the modern period,
for a variety of reasons, including both a sense that judgement is inconsistent with the love of God and the growth
of an expectation that all will be saved in the end, the last
judgement has become one of the most neglected of the
major eschatological images.

The New Testament uses the military image as well as
the law-court one. The former depends on the divine
warrior motif of the Old Testament: the God who defeats
his enemies and those of his people (see, e.g., Isa. 66:
15–16, applied to the parousia in 2 Thess. 1:7–8). But since
it is to execute justice that the divine warrior fights, he is
also judge (cf. Jude 14–15). In both images, God or Christ
enacts justice, whether as the judge sitting in judgement
and pronouncing the verdict of innocent or guilty (Matt.
25:31; 2 Cor. 5:10; Rev. 20:11–15), or as the royal warrior
who destroys the wicked and liberates the oppressed.

So in Revelation 19:11–21 Christ is depicted as the divine
warrior, coming to destroy his enemies in battle, but he is
also the judge (v. 11), whose fiery eyes penetrate to the
truth of human hearts (v. 12) and whose sword is the word
of his mouth condemning the wicked (v. 15). When the
forces of the beast are destroyed by the word of his mouth
(v. 21), the two images combine: are they killed by physical
violence or do they perish in the light of the divine verdict
exposing the truth of their lives? There is no need to
prefer one image to the other, precisely because both are
images. Neither *describes* what will happen at the end of
history; both give *imaginative expression* to the hope that
God must finally remove evil from his world before it can
be new creation. The alternation and combination of the
images serves to remind us that both are images.

The divine warrior motif most appropriately depicts

140

Jesus Christ's achievement of God's kingdom by victory over the forces of evil that oppose God's rule (2 Thess. 2:8; Rev. 19:11–21). In Revelation it is primarily the system of evil, the beast and his false prophet representing a political and military system inspired by supernatural evil, that is destroyed. People perish because they have thrown in their lot with the beast.

The alternative image of all humanity, dead and living, appearing before God's judgement seat or (in some of the texts) Christ's judgement seat has a different emphasis. It focuses on the exposure of the truth of each individual's life and the judicial evaluation of it. It is notable, however, that, just as the beast is the prime enemy in the eschatological battle, so, in one depiction of the final assize, it is to the fire prepared for the devil and his angels that the wicked are condemned (Matt. 25:41). The righteous inherit the destiny prepared for themselves, the truly human destiny (Matt. 25:34), for which their names have been written in the book of life (Rev. 20:12, 15), but the wicked are left to the fate they have chosen by identifying themselves with evil. Thus, although the last judgement has two outcomes in the key texts, they are not symmetrical, as the medieval doomsday paintings might lead us to suppose. One is the destiny for which God has created humanity, the other is the consequence of refusing that destiny and making an irrevocable choice of evil.

Another way of understanding this point is by way of the Gospel of John's paradoxical portrayal of Jesus Christ's relation to judgement. Since Jesus in his incarnate life is the truth of God made manifest in human history, the judgement of the last day is in a sense already taking place in people's response to him. Those who refuse to come to the light he would shed on their lives, choosing to pursue evil in the darkness, are already condemned. Jesus himself condemns no one. He came not to condemn but to save.

141

He embodies God's purpose for salvation for the whole world. Yet Jesus' message, his witness to God's truth, the same witness that leads those who believe in him into the truth, itself condemns those who reject it. At the final judgement, Jesus' message, whose purpose was salvation, will become a witness against – and so the judge – of those who built their lives on rejecting it (John 3:17–21; 12:46–48).

Thus the same purpose of God which intends salvation for all cannot but entail the condemnation of those who refuse it. The importance of this is in part that it enables us to see the biblical portrayal of God's purpose in Christ as consistent. That the same Jesus Christ should come first as Saviour, but finally as Judge has disturbed many contemporary Christians, but seems not to have been problematic at all for the New Testament writers. But God's saving purpose does not change from incarnation to parousia. The completion of that purpose, the bringing to light of the final truth of the lives of those who inherit eternal life, is accompanied inevitably by the bringing to light of the truth of the lives of any who have rejected the light.

Three important questions remain about the way the last judgement is depicted in the New Testament texts. One is the dualism of the portrayal. Why are there only two fates to which those tried are assigned? Since their whole lives are being assessed, should there not be a sliding scale of good and evil with rewards and punishments in corresponding gradations? The answer is that, although it is by their deeds that people will be judged, God's final judgement is not understood as a legalistic implementation of distributive and retributive justice. What is judged is the appropriateness of a life for entry into eternity. What the deeds expose is the fundamental alignment of a

142

person's self towards God and the good or, conversely, the fundamental rejection of God and the good.

Therefore judgement according to deeds is not inconsistent with the decisive nature of faith. The deeds are the index of faith or the lack of it. Nor does it exclude God's mercy. Far from it. No one could pass this assessment without God's limitless mercy. But even with God's limitless mercy no one whose fundamental choice has been made for evil can enter the eternal kingdom of God's righteousness. In the nature of the case they do not belong there. But those who, sinners that they are, have desired God's mercy, are shown, in the final truth of things which the last judgement brings to light, to be aligned towards God and his kingdom. They belong there.

Secondly, by what criterion is judgement made? Though the various New Testament witnesses portray this in various different ways, they are united in seeing relationship to Christ as in some way the criterion. Two ways in which we might think of this are as follows. One is in terms of Jesus' message of the coming of the kingdom of God, a message of radical grace and radical demand. He came to call sinners, not the righteous, but he calls them to a life of radical commitment to living the life of God's kingdom. That the verdict at the last judgement is both according to deeds and entirely dependent on God's mercy is consistent with this.

Another way of thinking of Christ as the criterion of the judgement is in terms of the cross. The crucified Christ bears already and representatively the full weight of God's final condemnation of sinners, but bears it in order that God's love might reach those under condemnation, bringing forgiveness and renewal of life. Those who by faith find in Christ their representative discover already, provisionally, God's verdict in their favour. The astonishing coincidence of God's utter condemnation of sinners and his radical grace for sinners occurs definitively in the cross and will recur at the last judgement. The last judgement will implement only what has been decided once and for all at the cross. From this perspective we can see that it is mistaken to think that God's judgement and God's mercy detract from each other, as though the more weight we give to judgement, the less we can give to mercy, and vice versa. Rather, there is direct proportionality between the two. God's mercy is as extensive as the severity of his judgement, and his judgement as uncompromising as the depth of his mercy.

Thirdly, cannot condemnation at the last judgement prove salvific? God's judgements in history have salvific intent: they expose the evil of which sinners must repent. May not this therefore also be true at the last judgement? So some have argued.[31] They see condemnation at the last judgement, the exposure of the evil of one's life such that one cannot but recognize it as evil, as a purgative process of painful repentance and renewal. The last judgement could then be seen as a key moment in a salvific process which might bring all to salvation in the end. But this is to reformulate the image in a way which is not true to the biblical usage of it. Unlike other forms of divine judgement, the last judgement is precisely *final*. It brings to light the fundamental alignment of a person's being as it becomes apparent in the whole course of their completed life. It pronounces a verdict on that completed life; it cannot change it.

But there is another way in which the last judgement can prove salvific. The only reason why the gospel message in the New Testament includes reference to the last judgement is so that it may serve the cause of that salvific message now. In the preaching of Jesus, for example, judgement is always a warning to avoid the path to final condemnation, a summons to decision and repentance.

144

Precisely because it cannot change people at the end, the last judgement, with its prospect of a time when it will be too late to repent, changes people now. Not to satisfy our curiosity as to universal salvation, but to face us with the serious possibility of finding ourselves finally condemned, is the purpose of the image in its biblical contexts. This does not mean that we are to live in fearful uncertainty of our future. The Christ who is coming in judgement himself bore the judgement in love for us on the cross. To live in the light of final judgement means to remember that our lives are lived under God's scrutiny, to realize that we shall never cease to need God's mercy in Christ, and to trust in the love that casts out fear.

In the following images we shall consider some of the ways the Bible and the Christian tradition picture the eternal bliss of those for whom the last judgement is their definitive entry into eternal life with God. But some mention should be made here of the antithetical images of final condemnation, depicting the fate of those who, in the words of the Gospel, share the destiny prepared for the devil and his angels. Whether any will make such a final choice for evil, throwing in their lot with the evil that God must finally remove from his good creation, is a different question – and one which many will wish to leave open – from the question of the seriousness with which these images must surely, on the basis of the biblical testimony, be taken.

In their New Testament usage, especially that of Jesus in the Gospels, these images bring before us the real possibility of final loss, not in order to scare us into a repentance which could not in any case be authentic were self-interested fear its only motive, but in order to shock us into realization of the moral and ultimate seriousness of the self-orientations of faith and life that align us either with God or against God. Yet, in the case of these images

145

no more than in the case of those which depict eternal bliss, should we try to reduce their imaginative variety to some literalistically conceived version of hell.

Behind much of the New Testament imagery of final condemnation lie Old Testament images of judgement, such as the paradigmatic fate of Sodom and Gomorrah, destroyed with sulphur and fire, and reduced to a permanently smoking waste (Gen. 19:24, 28; cf. Rev. 14:10–11), or the permanently worm-eaten and burning state of the last rebels against God in Isaiah (66:24; cf. Mark 9:43, 45), or the gnashing of teeth by the wicked when they see the righteous finally vindicated and blessed (Ps. 112:10; cf. Matt. 22:13; 24:51; 25:30). Most of the New Testament language depicts either final destruction (e.g. Matt. 10:28; John 3:16; 2 Cor. 2:15–16; 1 Thess. 1:9) or eternal torment (e.g. Rev. 14:11; cf. Matt. 18:8; 25:41, 46), but there are other images too, often combined with those two, such as exclusion and banishment from the presence of God and the bliss of the redeemed (e.g. Matt. 8:12; Luke 13:24–28; 2 Thess. 1:9; Rev. 22:14). The latter is not in literal terms compatible with the alternative image of suffering the wrathful presence of God (Rev. 14:10), another illustration of the way images must be read as images, not literal depictions.

What is clear from the use of all the images of final condemnation is that at least they depict the unimaginable horror of rejection by God and its finality. They do not suggest a limited judgement or a purgatorial experience from which people may eventually emerge to salvation. They represent the final loss of salvation. It may be that beyond this we cannot go. The traditional doctrine of hell took the images of eternally experienced punishment literally, but was thereby obliged to take the images of final destruction less literally. Our contention that eschatological language is irreducibly imaginative suggests that we should be content to let the various images stand, not reducing one to another, though we must also avoid understanding them in a way that is inconsistent with what we know of God and God's purposes in Christ. The literal reading of these images has in the past sometimes exercised a seriously distorting effect on believers' images of God, while conversely the modern tendency to exclude them altogether has helped to sap the seriousness from the biblical account of God's judgement.

THE GARDEN OF GOD AND THE CITY OF GOD

> The Garden – was it real or was it dream?
> Slow in the hazy light, I have been asking,
> Almost as a comfort, if the past
> Belonging to this now unhappy Adam
> Was nothing but a magic fantasy
> Of that God I dreamed.
>
> (Jorge Luis Borges)[32]

> The City is not a final term of flattery to our existent politics or a sanction of compromised politicians. This eschatological imagery, above all, lives by contrast rather than analogy.
> (Ulrich Simon)[33]

It has been said that the biblical story of humanity begins in a garden – Eden – and ends in a city – the New Jerusalem. This is only partly true, since the vision of the New Jerusalem in Revelation 21:2–22:5 also has Edenic characteristics (22:1–2). We could say that the biblical story begins in a garden and ends in a garden city. But to appreciate the significance we must be careful about the word 'garden'. Although Paradise does indeed mean 'garden', it is portrayed in the Bible as *God's* garden (Ezek. 28:13), not a garden made by humans. It is not, as we often think of human gardens, a garden by virtue of not

147

being wild nature. The garden God planted (Gen. 2:8) *is* wild nature – or at least it is nature as God first intended it to be. For Adam to be the gardener of *this* garden (Gen. 2:15) did not mean giving human order to nature but respecting its God-given order, not making something out of nature but caring for nature as God made it.

Adam and Eve in paradise are a picture of humanity in ideal harmony with the rest of God's creation. Their expulsion from Eden is their estrangement from nature. Eden is the lost dream of a natural world in which humanity can feel wholly at peace and at home, the dream from which human societies have so often felt themselves to have just awoken, wishing themselves back in it, the delight slipping from the memory as fast as they try to recover it. Again and again they have sought it in gardens of their own making[34] or in idyllic parts of wild nature or in nature recreated in art – the beauty of nature without its danger, the cornucopia without the thorns and the tempests, the bird song without the viper, the promise without the threat. And such approximations to Eden have been real enough and delightful enough to keep alive the nostalgia for Eden itself.

Yet Eden is more than the enchanted forest in which humans once belonged. It is the holy heart of nature. It is situated on 'the holy mountain of God' (Ezek. 28:14), at the mythical centre of the world, where not only humans and nature, but also God and humans and God and nature are at one. As such it is the life-giving heart of nature from which the life of the world is continuously derived and replenished. Down from the mountain of Eden runs the river of the water of life, dividing into four rivers that symbolically encompass the four quarters of the earth (Gen. 2:10–12). Eden is the source of the fertility of the whole earth from which all living things live. But away from Eden all life runs out in the end. All living things die. To live in Eden would be to live from the undying source of life. It would be to drink the water of life and to eat the fruit of the tree of life. In that sense humanity's loss of Eden was more the loss of a possibility than the loss of an actuality. The fiery sword of the cherubim barred them not so much from what they had had as from what they might have had: the eternal life that the tree of life represents (Gen. 3:24).

The scholars who pioneered the modern study of biblical eschatology left us the dictum: *Endzeit* (end-time) corresponds to *Urzeit* (primal time). How far this is true can be seen from the echoes of the first two chapters of the Bible in the last two chapters of the Bible. But the new creation is in every respect much more than the first. It is not just the perfection of the first creation restored after the damage evil has done it. It is the unrealized promise of the first creation finally achieved. Adam and Eve before the fall were innocent of evil, not morally perfect. They could and did sin, whereas humanity in the resurrection will be secure in their goodness, as God is, unable to sin.[35] Adam and Eve before the fall were mortal: it was possible for them to die and, exiled from Eden, they did. Immortality was an unrealized dream. In the new creation, death will be abolished, and all life, by virtue of its immediacy to God, the divine source of all life, will live eternally beyond the reach of death. In the biblical image, the inhabitants of the New Jerusalem will drink the water of life that flows from the throne of God and Christ, and the nations will eat of the constantly available fruit of the tree of life that grows on the river's banks (Rev. 22:1–2; cf. 2:7; 21:6; 22:17).

This kind of correspondence between *Urzeit* and *Endzeit* does not contradict our knowledge of humanity's evolutionary origins and prehistory. It finds in human beginnings not perfection, but the promise of perfection, the dream of what might be that historical humanity has

149

never been able to forget. The fulfilment will be in every respect more but in no respect less than the dream. Corresponding to the principle of theology that God is always greater than we can imagine is the principle of eschatology that the fulfilment God gives will always be better than we can imagine.

Since Eden humanity has lived amid the polarity of wild nature and city. Eden is the heart of the world conceived as nature, the city is the heart of the world conceived as human civilization. In the ancient world, the ideal city was the holy city at the centre of the earth, itself centred on the immediate presence of the gods in their temples, often perceived, like Eden, as the mountain of God, where the divine and the human meet. Expelled from God's life-giving presence at the heart of nature, humans sought God's presence again, blessing and inspiring human culture, at the heart of the city. Hence it is not only in the eschatological Jerusalem, portrayed in Revelation, that the city gains paradisal features. This is already the case in Old Testament accounts of the earthly Jerusalem which draw on mythical themes. Mount Zion, in historical reality a hill of only modest height, becomes in mythic perception the cosmic mountain towering over all the earth (Ps. 48:1–2; 46:4). In eschatological expectation such paradisal features are magnified (Isa. 2:2; Ezek. 40:2; 47:1–12; Zech. 14:8).

Not only Jerusalem was seen by its ancient inhabitants as the holy centre of the world. In the cities of the Mesopotamian plain artificial mountains – ziggurats – functioned as the home of the gods among humans. Genesis prefigures them in the story of the tower of Babel, the artificial cosmic mountain built by humans in their attempt to storm heaven and rival God (Gen. 11:1–9). Clearly in the Bible the city has an ambiguity Eden never had. At the centre of the city may be, not the presence of God, but idolatry

150

and human self-deification. After all, it was when Cain was expelled from the presence of God that he built the first city (Gen. 4:16–17). In the book of Revelation we encounter not only the New Jerusalem, but also the city it replaces: Babylon, the latter-day Babel, where power and profit, militarism and growth are the patron deities.

If the city has an ambiguous character in the biblical story, so does wild nature after Eden. It is the soil humans must sweat to make a living from (Gen. 3:17–19). Truly wild nature, uncultivated and untamed by humans, often appears in the Bible as hostile to human interests, a threat to human life and culture.[36] From this perspective – understandable enough in the realities of life for the Israelite peasant farmer – it is less obvious that the city is a threat to wild nature. But, as Evan Eisenberg points out, for the tower of Babel to have reached heaven, its base would have had to cover the earth[37] – an appropriate symbol of the way the economies of cities have increasingly subjugated the countryside and devastated wild nature, culminating in the city-dominated global economy of our own time. The worshippers of the beast, the consumers of Babylon, are 'those who destroy the earth' (Rev. 11:18).

The conflict of city and nature, which could at first be seen as the attempt to build a human world secure against the threat of wild nature, has come in our own day to the point where the city threatens to reduce nature to desert. The loss of Eden, the source of the life of wild nature, comes full circle in urban civilization's destruction of Eden. Since the urban centre of culture cannot live without the natural sources of life, the city's destruction of nature is self-destructive. Humanity can survive only if we live within the polarity of city and wild nature, resisting the domination of either over the other. In the last analysis we can do this only if we find God at the heart of both, escaping the compulsion to usurp the Creator's role and escaping the temptation to deify nature. Neither human culture nor nature is divine; both may be holy if we seek God in their midst.

In the cathedral church of Visby, on the Swedish island of Gotland, a modern stained-glass window[38] depicts the small city of Visby as the New Jerusalem. Well-recognizable features of Visby mingle with visual allusions to Revelation 21–22. There are twelve gates, the river of life runs through the centre of the city, and it is lit by the light that streams down on it from God the Trinity. In place of the Baltic which borders the real Visby, the city in the picture is surrounded by the heavenly sea of crystal mingled with fire. The picture stands in a long tradition. Many Protestant Bibles of the sixteenth century included an illustration of Revelation 21 in which the artist Hans Holbein had depicted the New Jerusalem as Lucerne, though in this case conforming the Swiss city to the text of Revelation only by stationing angels at the city gates. In the Visby window the city is a notably green one. Verdure is as much in evidence within its walls as buildings are. As an aspiration for the real city to live in the light of God and in as close conformity as possible with the ideal city that comes down from heaven, the window is inspiring.

However, it would be a mistake to suppose that a harmony of human civilization and wild nature can be achieved by the inclusion of nature within the city or even within the orbit of the city's control. Desirable as garden cities are, the heart of nature cannot be moved into the city and cannot survive the city's domination. In this world the city can never *coincide* with nature as the New Jerusalem does. The ideal city with the mythic qualities of Eden can only be a symbol of the reconciliation of culture and wild nature; the centre of each can only be one centre in the important sense that it is God who as the heart of both can reconcile the two. But the image of the New Jerusalem which is also Eden transcends this world as an image of the new creation. In being city as well as paradise, it takes all that is good in human culture after Eden through transformation into the eternal kingdom of God. It is paradise regained and also human culture redeemed.

As such it must also be the ultimate reconciliation of wild nature and human culture. It must be the place, not only where humans and God are at one and humans and nature are at one, as was the case in Eden, but also where human civilization is in harmony with wild nature, as has never been the case. Another biblical image of this, important because it puts the wild animals back with humans in Eden, is Isaiah's vision of peace on the holy mountain in the end (11:6–9; 65:25). This is not, as often supposed, merely a picture of peace within nature. It is a picture of peace between the human world, with its domesticated animals, and the wild animals that ancient Israelite farmers saw as threats to their lives and livelihood. Nor is this strictly a return to Eden, where there were no domesticated animals. It is a vision of that high mountain, already to be glimpsed in the eschatological future, where wild nature will come into its own without threat from us and we shall find our true place at last within the whole of God's creation.

SABBATH REST AND MARRIAGE FEAST

> There Sabbath unto Sabbath
>   Succeeds eternally,
> The joy that has no ending
>   Of souls in holiday.

(Peter Abelard)[39]

> From this Fountain
> flows the stream of the oil of gladness,
> which gladdens the city of God,
> and the powerful fiery torrent,
> the torrent, I say, of the pleasure of God,
> from which the guests at the heavenly banquet
> drink to joyful inebriation
> and sing without ceasing
> hymns of jubilation.
>
> (Bonaventure)[40]

In Fra Angelico's painting of *The Last Judgement* (c. 1431), some of the blessed in paradise are dancing.[41] The figures, alternately angels and people, join hands in what is evidently a round dance, though the circle is not complete. The picture evokes the ordered grace of medieval courtly dancing. Especially in combination with other figures who are embracing or engaged in conversation, the dance should be seen as an activity of shared joy and an expression of the joy of sharing. Perhaps the circle is incomplete because it is open to the inclusion of others. Some of the others are depicted as gazing in adoration upwards to the throne of God, which is surrounded by worshipping angels. (They are placed in contrast to the damned, who turn away in terror from the sight of God.) Adoration, fellowship and dance are what the blessed do in this vision of paradise.

Although dance is not explicitly a biblical image of eternal life, other images of social enjoyment (in which dance may well be implicitly included) are certainly biblical, especially the banquet (Isa. 25:6; Matt. 8:11; Luke 14:15) or the marriage feast (Rev. 19:9). It was with reference to this great festival of the world to come that Jesus said, at the last supper, that he would not drink wine again until the time when he will drink new wine in the kingdom

154

of God (Mark 14:25). Jesus' own custom of sharing meals not only with his disciples but also with notorious sinners (see, e.g., Matt. 11:19) is probably to be understood as part of his practice of the coming kingdom already in his ministry. It is at God's eschatological junket that those who now eat scarcely enough to stay alive will for the first time eat their fill, while those who now experience the tragedy of life will join fully in the general merriment (Luke 6:21; cf. Rev. 9:16). There will no longer be any cause of suffering, sadness or want, for God himself will wipe every tear from every eye (Isa. 25:8; Rev. 7:17; 21:4). In God's presence in the new creation there will be reason only for celebration and jubilation, and every reason for these.

In these images of festivity the world to come is contrasted with the suffering and sadness of this world. A parallel image contrasts the Sabbath rest of the world to come with the 'labours' of this world (Heb. 4:1–11; Rev. 14:13). The two images are not incompatible, as they might seem to those who have negative experiences or ideas of sabbatarian Sundays. On the biblical Sabbath what is prohibited is work, not enjoyment. Its rationale is not so much that people should rest in order to work, but rather that they should work in order to enjoy the blessing of the Sabbath day.

This is most apparent from the fact that the Sabbath is modelled on God's own example in resting after the six days of creation (Exod. 20:11). Having done his work, God rested in enjoyment of it. Hebrews understands this divine Sabbath rest as eschatological, as the rest that God will finally enjoy in the new creation. Only then will his creation, rescued by him from transience and evil, be perfected. This eschatological rest of God is the Sabbath that also awaits the people of God (Heb. 4:1–11), who will rest from the labours of their mortal lives and share God's joy in his completed creation for eternity. God will rest in

155

them and they in God. As C. S. Lewis puts it, 'Joy is the serious business of heaven.' [42]

Workaholics may not find this picture of eternal rest very attractive, but those who are fortunate enough to find their work pure pleasure should remember that we are dealing in images. The eschatological rest is from the exhausting toil required of most people in this life simply to keep themselves alive. We need not banish from our images of the world to come the kind of pleasure in creativity or reflection or service to others that work at its best provides. Rather, we should think of them as like the dance, the music-making, the laughter, the entertaining of each other that are suggested by the image of the eternal Sabbath feast.

We should also remember that in the biblical and Christian tradition, as in most cultures, festivity and worship belonged much more closely together than they do in western society today. Most of the annual festivals in Israel's calendar were occasions for celebration and feasting in the temple. Our own vocabulary reminds us of the time when holidays were also holy-days. So we need not distinguish too sharply between the images of festal merry-making and the images of worshipping God with music, singing and dance that also belong to the literature and iconography of the eschatological hope. The enjoyment of God in creative expressions of praise and glory will be the keynote of the party God himself is laying on for our homecoming. As Augustine expresses it, 'All our activity will be "Amen" and "Alleluia".'[43]

There is a further significance in the fact that the most common (biblical and traditional) images of what the blessed in the world to come will 'do' are images of enjoying beauty and playing games. These are activities whose value and meaning lie wholly in themselves, not in their contribution to the achievement of a further goal or purpose. Coherently with them, the Christian tradition has usually thought of eternal life in terms of final attainment and fruition. It is the goal towards which we aim in this life; in the life to come it will have been attained. Now on the road to perfection, then we shall have been perfected. Now in motion towards our destination, then we shall come to rest. The motif of the vision of God (which we shall consider in the final section of this chapter) has often been understood to mean that in eternal contemplation we shall mirror the changeless perfection of God himself.

This perspective in the tradition has not always been seen as incompatible with any sort of movement or progress in the eternal state,[44] but it is especially in the modern period that dissatisfaction with the 'static' image of eternal life as achieved perfection has grown.[45] This must reflect the general ethos of the modern period in the West. Modern people do not want to come to rest and to enjoy the fruit of their labours, because it is the struggle to achieve and the vision of further progress that really give pleasure. Modern people do not wish, like Augustinian humanity, to find in God the rest for their restless hearts; they want ever new worlds for their restless spirits to conquer. If there is 'heaven', it should not be the end of the road, weary humanity's homecoming, but rather like struggling over the brow of the hill to find a vast new vista of unexplored country ahead of us. The appropriate adage is: 'To travel hopefully is better than to arrive.'

The adage may be misleading. While it may be true that many achievements and attainments in this life prove ultimately unsatisfying in themselves, this may be precisely because they belong to this life. More relevant may be that we wish it were not so. The disappointment we sometimes experience in achieved hopes indicates a desire for an ultimately satisfying goal. Christian eschatology maintains that God himself is the goal for which we were created and which, once attained, will prove endlessly satisfying. If God is really God, it must be better to find God than eternally to seek God.

Moreover, if God is really God, there must be in the world to come the moral perfection which follows the elimination of all evil. If we are not destined for moral perfection and for satisfaction in the end of all temptation and moral struggle, then we should have to see evil as inherent in our created nature and an ineradicable feature of God's creation. The Christian expectation is rather that in the new creation all creation will be securely good, as God is, no longer threatened by evil, no longer morally precarious as it is in this world. Our participation in the life of God will ensure this.

In these important respects the eschaton means final and fully satisfying arrival in the eternal home for which we have always been destined. This is one reason why it necessarily transcends our present experience in ways that make it impossible to describe. But we can imagine movement that is not from bad to good, and therefore compatible with the kind of eschatological attainment we expect. The aesthetic images of music and dance may be particularly helpful here. The experience of movement and successiveness is integral to our enjoyment of such activities, but the movement is not progress from bad to good or even from good to better. Such activities can seem to have their own time, set apart from the ordinary time in which we envisage a future towards which we are moving. Like games, when sufficiently absorbing, their rationale is wholly in themselves and in their own time.

We may also recall the mystical moments of love or contemplation of beauty or worship of God which, though not actually outside time, can seem eternal and can seem so wholly satisfying we should like them to go on for ever. Such experiences enable us to glimpse the possibility of experiencing not timelessness, but a kind of time appropriate to the enjoyment of fruition. In eternity we shall no longer have goals towards which we must measure our temporal progress. In the worship whose only purpose is to please God and to enjoy God, we shall eternally lose ourselves in the beauty and love of God and eternally enjoy the surprise of finding ourselves in God.[46]

THE KINGDOM OF GOD

> The kingdom cannot be reduced to human expectations of the future any more than it can be reduced to human experience of the present. The temporal ambivalence of the kingdom in Jesus' preaching, its presentation as both present and to come, attests its transcendent character.
>
> (Bruce Chilton)[47]

> If the Kingdom comes, either it will be too much like itself to be livable, or it will become too livable to remain like itself. The Kingdom that has 'come' is already a new Exile in which to feed nostalgia for another Kingdom.
>
> (Henri Desroches)[48]

The image of the kingdom of God has particular significance for two reasons. One is that it is the eschatological image most used by Jesus in the Synoptic Gospels. Though not unimportant elsewhere in the New Testament, the phrase 'the kingdom of God' (and 'the kingdom of heaven', where 'heaven' is a periphrasis for 'God') is especially characteristic of Jesus' usage. The second reason this image has particular significance is that, more than any other of our ten images, it raises the question of the relationship between the eschatological future and the present. There are other ways in which we could have approached that issue: for example, through the image of eternal life as it is used in the Gospel of John (where it

159

takes over the role played by the kingdom of God in the Synoptic Gospels), or through the work of the Holy Spirit, understood, especially in Pauline theology, as the first instalment of the eschatological salvation which in its fullness is still to come. However, the kingdom of God is probably the most comprehensive image that in the New Testament refers both to the universal eschatological future and to the real anticipations of that future in the biblical story from the ministry of Jesus onwards.

(It is worth noting that most of the other images we have discussed in this chapter occur, even if very rarely, in the synoptic teaching of Jesus, where they are for the most part assumed as familiar images to which reference can be made without explanation. It is not difficult to see the kingdom of God in Jesus' teaching as the image that implies or includes all the other eschatological images to which he refers.)

The kingdom of God is, of course, a political image.[49] It is a political image of God's relationship to his whole creation, not just to his own people or to humanity as a whole, but also to the natural world. (What distinguishes it from the more limited image of the millennium – which, as we have seen, is also primarily a political image, evoking the victory and rule of Christ with his people on earth – is that the kingdom of God is a fully comprehensive image of the achievement of God's unlimited sovereignty over all things eternally.)

Especially in the Gospels, the kingdom of God is for the most part a dynamic term for God's ruling activity, though in some expressions, such as 'to enter the kingdom', it means something more like the sphere of God's rule. God's rule, for Jesus, does not suggest merely that God sits on the throne of the universe in heaven, but that he is actively at work in the world implementing his rule. The coming of the kingdom, now or at the end, entails God's victory

160

over all that is opposed to his will: evil, suffering, death, chaos and nothingness. Emphatically the kingdom is *God's* rule. It relates to and requires human activity – which can acknowledge and respond to it, pray for it and experience it, live in accordance with it – but it comes from God. It is God himself at work redeeming and perfecting his creation.

It is widely acknowledged that Jesus in the gospels speaks of the kingdom of God both as the decisive and impending future reality and as in some sense already active in the present in Jesus' own ministry. Jesus, as the one who speaks and acts with the authority of the coming God, enacts God's rule in his works of divine power, overcoming evil, sickness and death, and in his acts of divine grace, forgiving sins and welcoming the outcasts into God's presence. The clearest statement of the presence of the kingdom relates to Jesus' exorcisms: 'If it is by the finger of God that I cast out demons, then the kingdom of God has come upon you' (Luke 11:20), where the point is the overcoming of Satan's rule (11:18) by God's sovereign power in action. The exorcisms are instances of God's rule coming about. So also are the so-called nature miracles, such as the stilling of the storm, in which Jesus acts with the specifically divine power to command the sea and lays to rest the destructive forces which since creation have threatened to return God's creation to chaos. Also to be seen as instances of God's rule coming about are Jesus' meals with outcasts and sinners, in which Jesus shares the messianic banquet already with those who accept the invitation.

It should be noted that in all these activities Jesus not only *demonstrates* the coming of the kingdom but also *illustrates* what the kingdom is like and what difference it is making in the world, just as he also does in the parables of the kingdom. By his attention-grabbing activities and his engaging stories – each an image of the kingdom –

Jesus draws people imaginatively into the elusive reality of the kingdom, as it impinges in the present but can never be grasped.

The presence of the kingdom is never such as to diminish the expectation of its future coming. Those who are aware of its presence are precisely those who pray urgently for its coming. Those who experience it are precisely those who orient their lives towards its future. Jesus' enactments of its presence draw attention precisely to the impending reality of its coming in universal and unavoidable fullness. Its presence, here and there, now and then, in occasional acts and encounters of Jesus, is understandable only as the first glimmers of the coming dawn or as the seed for whose mysterious growth into corn the farmer must wait.

Jesus' parables of growth (the seed growing secretly, the mustard seed, the leaven)[50] should not be misunderstood in a modern progressivist sense as depicting an incremental expansion of the kingdom from small beginnings to universal reality. Their focus is on the contrast between the easily unnoticed present reality of the kingdom and its eschatological universality. The paradox is not explained by a modern understanding of biological development, suggesting an intelligible process of historical expansion, but left as mysteriously in God's hands as the growth from seed to plant was for the Palestinian farmer of Jesus' time. The concept of anticipation will serve us better in this connexion than that of progress. It is not that God's rule is bound to be more in evidence in later periods than in earlier. Nor is the presence of the kingdom to be assessed for its potential to continue advancing. The modernist prejudice that good is only worth having or achieving if it belongs to a process of incremental progress must be banished from our thinking about the kingdom of God.

Jesus' message and acts demonstrate and illustrate the

kingdom so that, already before it comes in fullness of power, people may respond to it and begin to live under God's rule. To such people, in Jesus' expression, the coming kingdom 'belongs' (e.g. Matt. 5:3, 10; Mark 10:14). The ethics of the kingdom which Jesus teaches are the radical demand God's rule makes of those who acknowledge it, the corollary of the radical grace with which God's kingdom reaches sinners as freely forgiving love. The intensity with which Jesus conjoins radical grace and radical demand in his preaching of the kingdom relates directly to the eschatological character of the kingdom. It is, as it were, the direct impact of the impending rule of God on Jesus' hearers.

Also very striking, in this connexion, is the way the impact of the kingdom, for Jesus, is in ordinary needs and requirements of daily living – the practical needs specifically of the leper or the disabled beggar, the pragmatics of loving one's neighbour or one's enemy, the universal need for daily bread and frequent forgiveness – just as Jesus' parabolic depictions of the kingdom mostly relate to the everyday experience of his hearers. While Jesus uses some of the common images of the eschatological future and takes, for example, the last judgement and its outcomes very seriously, he avoids for the most part detailed discussion of the end or the new creation. His concern is for the impact the coming kingdom has in the present. Often this is quite unspectacular, but, just as in Jesus' parables the ordinary often turns unexpectedly extraordinary, so in his expectations of human life lived in the light of the kingdom Jesus expects the ordinary to turn extraordinary. The presence of the kingdom is for the most part occasional, small-scale, everyday, but it makes a considerable difference to the everyday. For those who have eyes to see, but only for those, the coming transformation of all reality, its redemption from evil in the presence of God, is already at work.

For many contemporary readers the image of the kingdom of God is problematic. Rule or kingship suggests heteronomy, hierarchy, oppression. God as king suggests the divine despot who negates human freedom or the distant monarch who deals with us without involvement. That Jesus' preferred eschatological image can evoke such negative responses is undoubtedly a problem for contemporary appropriation of Jesus' eschatological teaching. But closer examination of the way the image of the kingdom of God functions in Jesus' teaching in relation to other images will go a long way to dissolving the problem.

It is a remarkable fact that, whereas Jesus in the Synoptic Gospels constantly uses the term 'kingdom of God', nowhere is he represented as calling God 'king'[51] or as making God the subject of the verb 'to rule'. This strikingly consistent usage sets the Synoptic Gospels apart from all extant Jewish literature, in which the term 'kingdom of God' is much rarer and reference to God as 'king' more or less common. Jesus seems to have made one Jewish usage ('kingdom of God') peculiarly his own, while deliberately avoiding its common correlative (reference to God as 'king'). We should also notice that, whereas rabbinic parables very frequently use the figure of a king to represent God, Jesus' parables rarely do so (only Matt. 18:23–34; 22:1–13; cf. Luke 19:12).

How is this linguistic practice to be explained? It seems that Jesus was at pains to avoid the implication that God rules in the way that earthly kings rule. Much of Jesus' teaching seems designed precisely to show how God's rule differs from earthly rule. In the age of the quasi-universal empires, which claimed divine authority, reference to God's rule had become for Jews a potent way of asserting the ultimate sovereignty of the God of Israel and the expectation that his righteous rule must replace the oppressive rule of the pagan empires. Jesus' use of the term 'kingdom of God' connects his teaching with this Jewish discussion in which the issue is universal dominion. But by avoiding the concrete image of God as king and preferring other images, notably father, Jesus shifts the focus much more to characterizing God's rule as radically different from that of earthly rulers. The issue is not just that God's rule should replace the rule of the pagan empires, nor even just that God's righteous rule should replace the oppressive rule of the pagan empires. More radically than his Jewish predecessors, Jesus wishes to portray God's rule as an alternative to earthly rule which is quite unlike all earthly rule.

The image of kingship – despite the Old Testament ideal of the king who secures justice for the oppressed – was hard to rescue from the sense of exploitative domination (cf. Mark 10:42). In the parables Jesus subverts expectations of kings and masters and employers by making the story turn on their surprising actions (e.g. Matt. 18:23–27; 20:1–15; Luke 12:37). Outside the parables, Jesus avoids calling God 'king' and privileges instead the other common Jewish description of God: 'Father'. The point is not, of course, that earthly fathers may not be oppressive, but that Jesus' hearers can more easily attribute generosity, compassion and practical caring to a father in relation to his children (e.g. Luke 11:11–13) than to a king in relation to his subjects. Whereas the king in the parable of the Unforgiving Servant acts as no one would expect a king to behave, the father in the parable of the Prodigal Son acts in a way that is understandable (though not necessarily expected) in a father, but would be incomprehensible in a king. The point is, then, that we cannot understand what Jesus meant by the term 'kingdom of God' from the term alone, but only by attention to the wide variety of ways in which Jesus characterizes God's rule by contrast with earthly rule.

The contrast is nowhere so clear as in Jesus' account of the kind of social relationships that are constituted by God's rule over the community of the disciples. In a series of highly distinctive rejections of current social structures and relationships, Jesus portrays a society in which none of the claims to rank and status which were taken for granted in his world has any place at all. The three most important instances of this concern slaves, children and the poor.

Making a direct contrast with the oppressive regimes of the Gentiles, which was itself a Jewish commonplace, hardly needing to be stated, Jesus draws an unparalleled conclusion as to the different way in which the society of God's kingdom should be constituted: 'You know that among the Gentiles those whom they recognize as their rulers lord it over them, and their great ones are tyrants over them. But it is not so among you; but whoever wishes to be great among you must be your servant, and whoever wishes to be first among you must be slave of all' (Mark 10:43–44; cf. Luke 22:25–26; Matt. 23:11). Echoes of this theme are found in several places in the gospels, but most important is the scene in John 13, where the personal example of his own adoption of the role of the slave, to which Jesus refers in Mark 10:45 and Luke 22:56, is acted out in the foot-washing. Washing feet, a frequent, everyday menial task, was, more definitely and exclusively than any other task, the role of the slave. It was what every free person axiomatically regarded as unthinkably beneath their dignity. Jesus enjoins the disciples to wash one another's feet (13:14) not as a mere symbol of humility, but as an actual concrete instance, the most telling possible, of how the disciples should relate to each other. The ordinary everyday requirement of washing feet they are to do for each other. If this is not beneath their dignity, nothing is.

So Jesus abolishes social status, not by giving all the disciples the status of master (then there would always be others, outside the community, to set themselves above), but by reducing all to the lowest social status: that of slave. In a society of slaves, no one may think him- or herself more important than others.

Equally strikingly original is Jesus' use of children to illustrate what God's rule requires (Matt. 18:1–4; Mark 10:13–16). The reason why one must become like a child in order to enter the kingdom is not because childlike trust is required or even because humility in the sense merely of a humble attitude is required, but because children had no social status. They and the disciples who must be like them are 'little ones' (Matt. 18:6) in the sense of lacking any power or importance in society.

The statement that the kingdom belongs to such as children (Mark 10:14) may help us with the parallel statement that it belongs to the poor (Matt. 5:3; Luke 6:20). These poor are not the ordinary people who had enough to live, though little more, and a reasonable security of life. They are the utterly destitute, dependent on the unpredictable chances of casual labour or on charity. They include the disabled beggars Jesus so often healed and the poor widow who put the pittance which was all she had into the temple collection box. Just as the kingdom belongs to the children who have no social status, so it belongs to the destitute who are at the bottom of the social and economic heap. As Dominic Crossan puts it, the kingdom is a 'kingdom of nobodies'[52] – the children and the destitute. If the kingdom belongs to them, others can enter it only by accepting the same lack of status.

Jesus reconstitutes society under God's rule by making the social nobodies and outcasts the paradigm to which others must conform. This is why it is difficult, though not actually impossible, for the rich to enter the kingdom (Mark 10:24–25). The instruction that those who can afford to give dinner-parties should not invite their relatives and friends, but the poor, the crippled, the lame and the blind (Luke 14:13), requires something more radical than generous charity. It means treating the destitute as one's social equals. On these terms, but only on these terms, Jesus did not confine the kingdom to the destitute, any more than he confined it to the children. He did very seriously privilege the destitute and the children, in order to deprive all others of privilege.

With these aspects of Jesus' teaching and practice we are as far as possible from the implication that God's rule authorizes that of human kings and governing élites. But this vision of the kingdom is clearly also opposed to the plutocracy and meritocracy that prevail in most contemporary western societies. Now, as then, it is among the followers of Jesus, who pray his prayer for the coming of God's universal rule, that the life of that kingdom must first be modelled in ordinary life if it is to have any wider effect.

THE VISION OF GOD

To see Thee is the end and the beginning,
Thou carriest us, and Thou dost go before,
Thou art the journey, and the journey's end.

(Boethius)[53]

[God] will be the goal of all our longings; and we shall see him for ever; we shall love him without satiety; we shall praise him without wearying.

(Augustine of Hippo)[54]

In much of the Christian tradition the image of humanity's

ultimate goal and fulfilment has been the vision of God (or the beatific vision). It is an image of the theocentricity of the Christian eschatological hope. Humans have been created to find our eternal fulfilment and joy in the vision of God. Creatures can have no completion or perfection in themselves alone, and human creatures will find their faculties of love, knowledge and enjoyment of beauty fully satisfied only in relation to God.

In its biblical usage the idea of the vision of God presupposes the inaccessibility of God to mortal human sight (John 1:18; 1 Tim. 6:16) and the numinous holiness of God such that no one can see God and live (e.g. Judg. 13:22). In the Bible's uninhibited anthropomorphism, it is the face of God that humans desire to see, since it is in looking into someone's face that one sees who they really are. (Biblical writers more naturally think of the face as revealing the person than of the face as a mask behind which one may hide one's true self.) Moses, than whom no Old Testament figure knew God more intimately, was permitted to see only God's back as he passed out of sight, a fleeting glimpse of the divine glory, not the vision of the divine face (Exod. 33:20). Who God really is he hears (Exod. 34:6–7) but cannot see. It is in this sense that the God who has never been seen becomes visible in the incarnation (John 1:18). In the human life of Jesus – in the face of Jesus Christ (2 Cor. 4:6) – is seen the true identity of God. Yet even this knowledge of God in Christ Paul can consider indirect, fragmentary and obscure in this life: 'now we see in a mirror dimly, but then we will see face to face' (1 Cor. 13:12).

To the biblical hope of the eschatological vision of God (Matt. 5:8; Rev. 22:3–4) there are probably two kinds of background. One is the notion of seeing God in the temple (Ps. 17:15; 24:6; 27:4; 84:7). In the inaccessible darkness of the holy of holies, where the presence of God was

169

represented by nothing that could be seen but only by the empty space above the cherubim, YHWH's invisibility to mortal eyes was powerfully symbolized, by contrast with the visually impressive images of the pagan gods in their temples. Nevertheless Israelite pilgrims to the temple expected in some sense to 'see' God in the beauty and mystery of the temple rites. But Israel came to expect a more adequate fulfilment of this hope in the heavenly or eschatological temple, where God is present to his worshippers in immediate vision such as mortals cannot bear. The God who has no earthly image will himself be seen. Canonically, the psalms have been read in this eschatological sense (see Ps. 24:4–6 with Matt. 5:8).

Since the heavenly temple is also the throne-room of God the king, this liturgical background to the vision of God readily converges with a political image. In the oriental court, the king was normally inaccessible, but his close personal attendants were privileged to enjoy his immediate presence. So, in the New Jerusalem, which has no temple because God and Christ are present as its temple, his servants will worship him on his throne and see his face (Rev. 22:2–3). The biblical image of seeing God thus combines the sense of being in the immediate presence of God and of knowing God in his true identity. This 'face to face' knowledge, knowing God as we are known by God (1 Cor. 13:12), is not a purely intellectual matter but the involvement of the whole person in the fullest relationship with God of which humans are created capable.

In the ancient world Platonic philosophy also aspired to the vision of God. Its influence on Christian spirituality and theology in the patristic and medieval periods promoted a more purely intellectualist and individualist understanding of the vision, as intellectual contemplation of eternal being, anticipated in this life in solitary mystical ecstasy.

Tensions arose between this eschatological goal as inherently solitary, the alone with the Alone, and the more social and corporate aspects of the Christian hope, as also between this goal of the disembodied human reason absorbed in knowledge of God and the more holistic understanding of human destiny which bodily resurrection suggests. In Christian life before death it encouraged the Greek distinction between contemplation and action, felt, as in Plato, as a dilemma. The pursuit of the vision of God in the contemplative life, requiring withdrawal from society, seemed in tension with the practice of neighbourly love in the active life.

The image of the vision of God thus poses the issue of a polarity in Christian views of eternal life between theocentricity and anthropocentricity. Must human destiny be conceived either as the fulfilment of the individual exclusively in God or as the heavenly perfection of human relationships and society? Is the vision of God necessarily so overwhelmingly satisfying that any enjoyment of creatures becomes in eternity inconsiderable by comparison?[55] Or is the vision of God an inhuman goal, the aspiration of misanthropic hermits and intellectuals? Those who see an inevitable tension between the theocentric and the anthropocentric hopes of eternity recognize that few if any Christian depictions of eternal life have opted exclusively for one or the other, but detect an unstable balance and a constant swing of the pendulum towards one or other pole.[56] Historically this has often been the case, but need it be so?

The problem arises from the assumption that attention to God is exclusive of attention to creatures, or vice versa. Though this may often or even usually be the case in this life, it is an imperfection of this life that we may expect to be surpassed in eternity. God is not simply another reality alongside and competing with that of creation. God is in a significant sense the all-inclusive reality – not in the pantheistic sense that everything is God, but in the theistic sense that all things are God's creatures and possess their own truth and value precisely in their relationship to God. The creature cannot be truly and fully known and valued except as God's creature. God himself is known and loved in the true knowledge and love of his human and other creatures. For this to happen, it is necessary for God also to be known and loved for himself alone, apart from creatures, and so the paths of Christian spirituality have often included a discipline of weaning oneself away from the exclusive love of creatures for themselves. The aim, however, is not the rejection of creation but learning to love the creation 'in God', i.e. as it really is, as God's creation. Then creation is known and loved in God while at the same time, without contradiction or tension, God is known and loved in his creation.

It was Augustine in the penultimate chapter of his *The City of God* who offered the often neglected clue to understanding the eternal vision of God as inclusive, rather than exclusive of knowing and loving creation. In this world it is possible to ignore the relationship of creation to God. The heavens declare the glory of God and human life reflects the grace of God, but only for those who have ears to hear and eyes to see. Creatures can be known without reference to God. But in the new creation the creatures in their redeemed perfection will all reflect God precisely in being their own true reality. God will be seen in the neighbour and in the non-human creation as truly, though not in the same way as he will be seen in himself. Eternal life will be theocentric because the reality of creation is theocentric and will then be unambiguously and joyously so.

In the modern period the most appealing form of the eschatological hope has undoubtedly been the perfect human society, while more recently the ecological desire for a reconciliation of human society with nature has augmented that hope. By comparison, the hope of the eternal vision of God is alien both to modernity and to postmodernity. Yet the healing of human society and its relationship to nature requires precisely the recovery of this alien desire for God. Humanity cannot be truly human without God. Humanity cannot relate rightly to the rest of creation until both are understood as creatures of God. Without God as the all-inclusive goal of human life, such that all else is loved in God and God loved in all else, human loves and aspirations are perverted into idolatry. God as the eschatological goal of all things does not diminish the human, the creaturely and the natural, but quite the contrary: God alone gives them their true reality now and in eternity.

6

∞∞∞∞∞∞

Breaking the Spiral: the State We're in and the Possibility of Progress

Many are the words we speak
Many are the songs we sing
Many kinds of offering
But now to live the life

Help us live the life[1]

In a book concerned mostly with looking forwards to what is to come, there may yet be merit in beginning a chapter focused on what is by glancing backwards to what has already been! Throughout this book we have emphasized the need for Christian faith and theology to rediscover the transcendent horizon of its hope. Eschatology, we have argued, has finally to do not with the best that we can hope for in this world, but with a new world which will be brought into being only when God wills and acts to do so. The 'last things', therefore, are properly things which lie wholly beyond the sphere of natural and historical development or understanding. The conditions for them will not be looked for or found in any human achievement or evolutionary transition, but will be created by God himself out of the abyss of non-being on the cusp of which our world and its inhabitants exist precariously from moment

174

to moment, and into which they constantly threaten to topple apart from God's gracious and patient preservation.

Of course we cannot know this for sure. It cannot be demonstrated in the way that scientific theorems can. In all sorts of ways it is counter-intuitive and contradicted by the ways in which we habitually experience the world. Precisely because it lies beyond the legitimate range of our science we cannot 'know' it at all in the ordinary sense. Like any other view of what lies in our ultimate future it is finally a matter of faith, rooted in and nurtured by a long tradition of Christian imagining, and belonging to the category of those things 'revealed' to faith in one way or another. As we have seen, this revealing is closely tied to images deployed in Christian Scripture and the interpretation of these within the church. Within this living tradition, where the risen Christ himself is present and active through the Holy Spirit, the truth conveyed by these images is 'known' in another significant sense; namely, through the moral conviction which attends to our basic beliefs, things which we 'know' to be true even though we cannot explain how, and which themselves furnish a matrix which shapes our day to day knowing and acting in the world. Belief that the world is not finally driven by forces of 'motiveless, purposeless decay',[2] for example, functions in just such a way to shape our expectations, our desires and our actions (as, presumably, would its alternative should anyone take it fully seriously). Belief that the purpose, the *telos*, the end of this world lies beyond itself in another, continuous with it in some respects yet incommensurable in others, is closely related and shares a similar status and function, directing our imagining beyond the ambiguities of the here-and-now and thereby offering a meaningful framework for the living of life *in* the here-and-now.

In an age when the secular eschatologies represented by

the myth of progress in its various guises have all but fizzled out, a transcendent rather than an immanent horizon for hope offers the only adequate antidote to the alternatives of inert despair and a frantic hyperactivity.[3] In a more optimistic era the other-worldly orientation of Christian hope struggled to survive due in part, at least, to its relevance being less apparent. Perhaps it will prove to be the case that post-modern nihilism grants that relevance a higher profile. This is not, of course, simply to make a virtue out of contemporary necessity. The prophets had neither read Nietzsche nor, for all their divinely inspired foresight, anticipated the slide of modernity into hopelessness; yet they already sensed that, the world being as the world is, the ending of the myth of Babel is unlikely ever to be rewritten no matter how clever or technically skilled humankind may become. The state we are in today has its distinctive features to be sure; but in certain respects it resonates with the human circumstance across the centuries and millennia and across widely differing cultures. The biblical authors may not have faced the wonders and terrors afforded by advances in nuclear or genetic science, yet they were shrewd judges of the human condition, and they believed firmly that the human hope for salvation lay finally not in technology, politics, culture or nature, but in God's promise to make all things new. If our context clears the ground and allows their voice to be heard more clearly and taken more seriously, then so much the better.

SHOULD WE BOTHER PLANTING TREES?

There is, though, one rather obvious response to all this other-worldly emphasis; namely, does it not risk (perhaps even appear to warrant) an inappropriate attitude towards the present, towards this world in which we live in the meanwhile? If our sights are firmly fixed on something other and better than the here and now, that is to say, are we not likely to place too little value on the world we have and, as a consequence, treat it with disrespect or worse? If redemption, when it comes, will not be as a direct result or develop out of anything which we do (or do not do) now, if it will occur in spite of anything we do (or do not do) now, then surely we can do as we like in the meanwhile, and have no serious reason to struggle for anything better than we currently have? Does other-worldliness not always have this-worldly indifference, acquiescence and even libertarian excess as its price tag?

The converse certainly appears to be true. The gradual erosion of belief in a transcendent other-worldly future (which has its roots as far back as the humanism of the Renaissance) has coincided with a growing human concern with this world for its own sake.[4] This is manifest in the typically modern loves for science (understanding how this world works and how best to control its forces to serve our interests), art (celebrating the beauty of the sensory for its own sake rather than as a means to transport us into or fit us for some 'divine' realm), politics (seeking strategies to improve the material and economic conditions under which people currently exist) and other properly 'secular' concerns. The basic attitude is captured in the constant bids made by medical science to elongate the span of our individual lives (no matter what the quality of such elongation may prove to be) on the assumption that death is the worst thing that can happen to us. If we think 'this' is all there is, after all, then we are much more likely to value it while we have it, and seek to have as much of it as possible.

This no doubt accounts in part for the ever more stress-filled existences we enjoy: knowing (through the marvels of technology) so much more about our world than any previous generation has known, we are aware of just how

177

much there is to see and to do and to try, how much we are missing. Like visitors to an art gallery who arrive 20 minutes before closing time we rush from exhibit to exhibit, fearful that we shall miss something worthwhile. The horizon of our own finitude haunts us, and we rush to cram as much as we possibly can into the available space, travelling ever faster and further, seeing and tasting more, trying out as many options as we can while we have the time and, ironically, as a consequence having time for very little at all. Has there ever been a generation with so little time actually to take time and to enjoy the world? Always craving the next thing we so often fail to savour the moment offered to us.[5]

Notwithstanding all this, it is surely one of the distinct gains of the modern spirit to have learned better to appreciate this world and all that it grants us? Even though this appreciation has been ambivalent, and has brought us close to the brink of nuclear and ecological catastrophe in recent decades, the genuine gains associated with it are ones we should not wish now to surrender. If, though, the intellectual context for such a positive concern for this world was the effective relocation of the 'vortex of man's being from the future life to this',[6] is an other-worldly eschatology such as the one we have espoused here capable of sustaining it, or is it bound to rob it of vital energy?

There is little doubt that other-worldly preoccupation has often sapped the strength of a proper concern for the here and now within Christianity. In part this was due to alliances formed early between the gospel and classical philosophy, the latter's effective disparagement of historical existence being neatly summed up in Socrates' judgement that companionship with the body 'disturbs the soul and hinders it from attaining truth and wisdom' and his description of true philosophy as a meditation on and preparation for death when this hindrance would

finally be removed.[7] Of course this is a quite distinct kind
of 'other-worldliness', focusing on a dualism between tem-
poral/physical and eternal/spiritual existence rather than
a distinction between this world and the next; but it is a
pattern with which Christian theologians flirted from very
early in the church's history, and which Christian theology
has often reproduced, often in less sophisticated versions
than Plato's own. The persistence among Christians of
belief in an 'immortal soul' which is separable from and
survives the body, being in effect 'the bit which really
matters', is adequate testimony to this fact.

We must not lay the blame wholly at the door of extra-
Christian influences however. The entirely 'biblical' sentiments of the apostle Paul, according to whom 'we know
that while we are at home in the body we are away from
the Lord' whereas 'we would rather be away from the body
and at home with the Lord',[8] seem at first sight to lean in
a similar direction. Paul's desire is not for a bodiless
existence as Socrates' was, but rather for the embodied
existence of the resurrection; nonetheless he does articu-
late a clear preference for the 'there-and-then' over the
'here-and-now'. The same theme crops up again and again
in devotional writing across the centuries. So, for
example, in James Montgomery's hymn from the early
nineteenth century we find the following:

> Here in the body pent,
> Absent from Him I roam,
> Yet nightly pitch my moving tent
> A day's march nearer home.
>
> My Father's house on high,
> Home of my soul, how near
> At times, to faith's foreseeing eye
> Thy golden gates appear!
> Ah, then my spirit faints

179

To reach the land I love,
The bright inheritance of saints,
Jerusalem above.[9]

The words hardly suggest a strong affective attachment to the writer's present lot! Yet such sentiments need not be taken to devalue the here-and-now except in relative terms, and some such relative judgement would seem to be involved in the idea of salvation itself. That 'heaven' will be an improvement on this world, we must suppose, is part of what makes it heavenly. Nor should we forget that for many of those who have made the comparison life in this world, if not always 'nasty, brutish and short', was nonetheless altogether less comfortable than it is for most of those who will read this book. Modernity has made it easier for its citizens to appreciate the good things in life by setting limits to many of its more unbearable aspects. Yet Christians have sometimes devalued the this-wordly in a far more problematic way, not least in the context of looking forward to a future which wholly transcends it, and, ironically, not least in modern, western Protestant versions issuing from the midst of the best and most comfortable situations that this world has to offer.

So, for example, writing about North American apocalypticism of various sorts, Craig Nessan notes how it

> guards a relatively comfortable status quo for an affluent majority who are satisfied with their present circumstances. Since God is the one who is in control of the imminent end-time events, there is nothing about the future we are obligated to change. We need not alter social structures so the hungry are fed or conflicts are resolved nonviolently. Instead, we fulfil our obligation to the future by spreading the message about the signs of the end so that individuals will repent, accept Jesus, be saved, and themselves begin to spread this message to others.[10]

By stressing the essentially other-worldly and individual shape of Christian hope and God's sole responsibility for realizing it, Nessan argues, such trends wholly undermine any sense of personal commitment to the common good or 'responsible partnership in shaping the future God intends for human history'.[11] The attitude is nicely summed up in a bitter parody of it offered by a (non-Christian) observer: 'To Hell with this. This lot's going to Hell. Let's get the Hell out of here!'

All this is a long way removed from the sentiment often ascribed to Martin Luther according to which, were he to discover that the world would end tomorrow, he would go out into the garden and plant a tree. This is the vital question with which this chapter will be concerned. What should we do in view of the coming end of the world and God's promised creation of a wholly new one? Whether the end be tomorrow, in the year 2000 (as many apocalyptically minded Christians seem to suppose), or 2000 years from now; if it is coming at all, and nothing we do in the meanwhile will affect the final state of things, how should we then act, and why?

THE POSSIBILITY OF PROGRESS?

In what remains of this chapter we shall offer an alternative account of the relationship between other-worldly ('apocalyptic') hope and this-worldly commitment within the pattern of Christian faith. Picking up on and developing themes introduced in Chapter 3 we shall suggest that hope of a properly *transcendent* sort (i.e. hope which is invested in something lying beyond the horizons of nature and history and requiring a decisive new creative act of God to establish it) is not only compatible with but actually furnishes the most adequate source of and resources for action designed to transfigure the here-

and-now. All that we have said about the death of the myth of progress and its undue optimism must stand. There is a significant difference, though, between the typically modern adherence to progress as a *dogma* (as if progress were a law of nature identifiable in physical, biological and spiritual processes across the cosmos and, occasional blips notwithstanding, moving inexorably towards a utopian future) and the belief that, while in global terms stasis and even regress may be just as characteristic if not more characteristic of the world, nonetheless progress is *possible* within certain contexts and limits.[12]

This belief in the possibility of progress is necessary to undergird any meaningful striving for change towards something better. It is not sufficient for this purpose, though, and needs to be supplemented by another: namely, that such progress is *worth* striving for, given its limited nature and, in the strict sense, its being unnecessary for the achievement of redemption. We shall suggest that part of what it means to be Christian, a follower of the Christ, is to be committed to living history differently, pursuing the characteristic marks of the kingdom of God as Jesus describes and embodies these (truth, goodness, justice, peace, holiness, etc.) *in* this world even though God's kingdom itself is not *of* this world. We are called to do so not as a means to secure our (or the world's) salvation, but treating these moral goals as ends in themselves, things which are inherently worthy of pursuit within history and represent a valuing of this world and this life in their own right. The proper reason for feeding the hungry, healing the sick, comforting the distressed, protecting the weak and vulnerable, and so on, is not in order to provoke (let alone assist or enable) God to save the world, but because these are things which are worth doing and which ought to be done if we truly value life in the here-and-now. They are, we might say, concrete parables or anticipations of God's kingdom, the new creation, under the conditions of this world. To view them otherwise, as rendering the necessary conditions for or as even in some sense identical with the advent of this new order, is both to miss the radical newness of God's promised future and to fall into the very worst sort of personal, political and ecological works-righteousness.

Talk of 'striving', while far from inappropriate, is misleading if we do not inquire into the conditions under which alone the possibility of progress exists. Just as we are unable, through our own unaided effort, to bring about the new creation so, we shall argue, the hope for progress within this world is best understood as rooted (explicitly or anonymously) in a sharing in the power of God's transcendent future as made manifest in the present. In Christian terms this is explicitly identified as a participation in Christ through the power of God's Spirit of holiness. More generally, though, it might be described as living differently under the renewing influence of an essentially open future, rather than living within the constraints afforded by the consequences of the past. Wherever the forces of sin and death are resisted or overcome the Spirit of Life (who is none other than the Living God made known in Jesus Christ) may be identified at work constantly renewing his creation. Whether he is recognized or acknowledged as the source may not be a matter of indifference, but it is not decisive for the efficacy of his initiatives. There are complex issues of human freedom and divine action lurking not far from the surface here, but it is vitally important to be able to affirm God's renewing activity outside the boundaries of the Christian church as well as within it. This activity, we are suggesting, is best construed not as breaking in 'from above' so much as reaching back into the present from a transcendent future and drawing us, in various ways, towards that future

by generating unexpected and often surprising anticipations of it *within* the confines of a world over which the
power of death otherwise holds sway. It is through our
active sharing in these initiatives alone that 'progress' –
movement towards 'life in all its fullness' in its moral,
spiritual, physical, intellectual, economic or whatever other
dimensions – is possible, and we may hope for more in
the future than 'the desolate vision of "eternal return", of
all history as gyre and *deja vu*'.[13]

THE BLACKMAIL OF TRANSCENDENCE

It is hardly true to suggest that other-worldliness has usually
been characterized by a concomitant indifference towards
the things of this life. Such a statement is far too sweeping
and undiscriminating. It is a fact that people have regularly
allowed their expectations of 'the last things' to modify
their behaviour, sometimes with the oddest of results; but
attentiveness to the concerns of this world feature just
as prominently as negligence of it. So, for example, pre-
millennial fears and expectations through the year 999
produced a spate of examples on both sides, and we might
reasonably expect some similar pattern to surround the
passing of the second millennium into the third. In 999,
for example, expectation that history was about to come
to an end with the one thousandth anniversary of Christ's
birth led many to a temporary shift of focus from material
to more ultimate concerns. 'Buildings of every sort were
suffered to fall into ruins. It was thought useless to repair
them, when the end of the world was so near.'[14] Our own
day has already seen striking examples of the willing
neglect or abandonment of the physical trappings of
history by those convinced that some cataclysm was about
to sweep them away to a 'spiritual' Nirvana. The mass
suicide linked to the arrival of comet Hale Bopp in our

skies in 1997 is just one example of a phenomenon which, while perhaps more surprising in our own day than in earlier centuries, nonetheless fits an identifiable pattern of eschatological behaviour.

On the other hand, apocalypticism of one sort or another has also produced a fervent attention to the state of this world as, with the approach of some perceived end, turning point or judgement, houses are hurriedly put in order and accounts balanced. A thousand years ago, for example, there was a pattern of literal 'housekeeping' in order to prepare for the parousia. 'Rich men surrendered wagonloads of jewels in the hope that Christ would find them in a state of grace. Debts were revoked; convicts were let out of prison.'[15] Contemporary versions of this same attitude might be identified, for example, in some strands of New Age religiosity according to which the current moral, intellectual and ecological crisis of humankind represents the final death throes of one stage in the evolution of life or Spirit, a stage from which we may emerge on to a higher 'spiritual' plane of being, but only if, in the meanwhile, we put our house in order and avert the catastrophe which otherwise threatens to destroy us.

Seizing our ultimate destiny as *homo spiritualis* thus entails radical commitment in the present to a new human agenda: protection of the environment; careful consideration for the well-being of other, non-human, occupants of our planet; the transformation of economic, political and social institutions in the direction of more decentralized and relational models; the eradication of injustice; the promotion of non-violent processes in the resolution of disputes. These and other very this-worldly concerns are the route and the means to the discovery of our true humanity, both as individual persons and as a race. Their pursuit by sufficient numbers, albeit thinly spread throughout society, will finally result in an irreversible evolutionary shift which will transfigure the whole of reality from the innermost recesses of the individual soul to the farthest flung corners of the physical cosmos. As one classic New Age text has it: '*It can all be otherwise. . . . Our pathology is our opportunity.*'[16] The point is, of course, that it is up to us to *make* things otherwise, to avert catastrophe and prepare ourselves and our world instead to embrace its utopian alternative. It's a huge responsibility, and we are running out of time.

These latter examples actually evince little serious valuing of this world for its own sake. In one way or another they all grant decisive privilege to the future in a way which, as we have already suggested, is not true of the Christian hope for a new creation.[17] They are probably best understood as penitential enthusiasm designed to avoid the perceived future consequences of prior neglect and malpractice; but they do demonstrate that, whatever the motive, focus on the next world can have positive, as well as negative, practical results in this.

This same pattern is familiar enough within the sphere of personal, rather than cosmic, eschatology as it has often been understood within the church. Each of us faces a personal crisis towards which our lives move inexorably even though we often deal with it through the mechanism of repression, only facing and adjusting to its reality late in the day. In this way the shape of our individual lives mimics the overall shape of history: marked by transience rather than endurance, they must finally pass into a meaningless abyss of nothingness or else be transfigured into something new and better. If the Socratic approach was to seek death out and to welcome it as an escape from the shackles of the body, the Christian attitude has always been far more ambiguous, and this for several reasons. One is the intrinsic value which Christian faith recognizes in the material world which God has created. Even when life is at its hardest and most cruel the eye of faith has always wanted to echo the divine judgement of creation's dawn that, nonetheless, in some sense 'it is good',[18] rather than bad or a temporary hindrance to be overcome. Thus, from a Christian perspective, 'The notion that this life is no more than a preparation for a life beyond, is the theory of a refusal to live, and a religious fraud. It is inconsistent with the living God, who is "a lover of life".'[19]

Another reason why Christians have often been more enthusiastic about Socrates' 'shackles' than he was himself has to do with the dualistic shape which Christian expectation has assumed for most of the church's history. In other words, being less confident than many Christians today appear to be that the scope of God's salvation must finally include all persons without exception, many have wavered in their assurance about their own inclusion and, losing sight of the fundamental Christian conviction that God offers his salvation freely and without condition to all who seek it, have laboured under a fear which prefers to remain in this world as long as possible in order both to defer a potentially awful discovery, and to put their personal house in order and thereby possibly improve the eschatological odds in their favour.

The construal of this life as a period of probation after which we discover whether or not we have 'made the cut' for the next round has certainly gripped the Christian imagination over the centuries, and has frequently been exploited precisely because of its capacity to affect people's patterns of behaviour and agenda of priorities. Hell-fire sermons, detailing the torments awaiting those who fail to make the grade, have often been designed not so much as a form of perverse and self-righteous gloating, but rather as a genuine and well-intentioned attempt to scare the hell out of people and bring them into line with God's demands for human life, making them suitable for

187

salvation in the process. It is a curious fact that human imagination has always found it easier to deal with hell than with heaven, and, as George Steiner notes, to furnish concrete approximations to it in this world because 'the pictures had always been more detailed'.[20] Ironically, this may have something to do with the perceived usefulness of hell as a deterrent or reformative tool, dangling people over the imagined pit with its burning fires and horrors in order to avoid the likelihood of them actually having to face the reality of these things in due course. Even when belief in the objective reality of hell itself began to slip among the church's intelligentsia, the need to preach its reality and thereby maintain belief in it among the masses was sometimes urged on the basis that the erosion of such belief could only lead to moral laxity on a dangerous scale.[21]

Exploiting the connection between morality in this world and belief concerning the next has not, though, been the preserve of the much maligned 'hell-fire and damnation' preacher. Appreciation of its possibilities is found in far more sophisticated versions and the most surprising of places. So, for example, the philosopher of the German Enlightenment, Immanuel Kant, whose name is synonymous with the advocacy of reason in the face of all superstition, gave full recognition to the vital regulative role which eschatological symbols perform in relation to personal morality. While, therefore, he held that belief in an afterlife could not be a dogma (since it could not be known by reason) he insisted that such belief nonetheless played a crucial practical role. On the one hand it encouraged those who found within themselves a disposition to approximate to the absolutes of the divine law, assuring them that persistence in such effort was worthwhile since it would lead duly to an extension of this same rising moral curve into eternity. On the other hand, those whose lives

were on a downward spiral would find themselves provoked, under the threat of their moral torpor being set
into an eternal pattern, 'to make a break with evil so far
as is possible'. The symbolic representations of heaven and
hell, reward and punishment, Kant argues, are 'powerful
enough to serve to one part [of humanity] as reassurance
and confirmation in the good, and, to the other, for
rousing conscience to judgment, . . . hence as incentives,
without any necessity to presuppose *dogmatically*, as an item
of doctrine, that an eternity of good or evil is the human
lot also objectively'.[22]

Kant assumes that, while human beings must in theory
be able to attain to that which God's law demands, in
practice all will fall short of it in this life to one degree or
another. The practical function of eschatology, therefore,
is to galvanize their striving in the right direction either
by encouragement or threat. 'True religion is not to be
placed in the knowledge or profession of what God does
or has done for our salvation, but in what we must do to
become worthy of it.' In the interests of morality, therefore,
the sacred symbolic narrative 'should at all times be taught
and expounded'.[23] While Kant insists elsewhere that the
only true foundation for obedience to the law is an
unselfishness and unconditional response to duty,[24] the
'incentives' described in the passage cited (and Kant's
accompanying observations on the antinomian consequences of assurance[25]) amount to a legalistic account in
which self-interest mediated through the evocation of fear
appears to play a large part.

That the connection between personal eschatology and
patterns of behaviour in this life is strong, then, is unde-
niable. Many readers will have known someone who, upon
the discovery, realization or belief that their life was
drawing close upon its end, was impelled to some fundamental reordering of values, priorities and desires. In some

cases this may have resulted in sudden and dramatic changes of personality and transformed relationships. Nothing focuses the mind on the quality of life quite like death, especially one's own. The truth is that our society, for all its prurient fascination with the mechanics of death (served, as this is, by a growing barrage of video simulation) finds nothing more difficult than facing death itself and has largely banished it from public life.[26] In earlier ages a sudden and unexpected death was a highly undesirable thing precisely because death was something to be prepared for carefully in one way or another; but the notion of 'dying well' has long since disappeared in our society together with any widely held public belief in personal survival of death. Today the ideal for many is to die quickly and, preferably, unconscious of the event.

Kant's account of the role of eschatological symbolism in human living is, in effect, as the facilitator of an extension of 'preparation for death' throughout the whole of life. In this respect it offers a much more adequate vision, in Christian terms, than the last minute u-turns of so-called 'death bed conversions'. If we root ourselves in the teaching of Jesus then we shall find plenty to support the idea that the whole of life should be lived daily in the light of what lies at its end and beyond it, whether in personal or cosmic terms. Kant's account, however, with its eschatological carrot and stick, while it represents a sophisticated version of an idea widespread in both Protestant and Catholic teaching, and while textual support for it may certainly be quarried from both Old and New Testaments, is finally a distortion of the way Scripture as a whole thinks about the impact of eschatological hope in transfiguring the lived present.

Kant is faithful enough in his presentation of the absolute holiness which Scripture presents as characteristic of God. He understands only too well the apparent awfulness of this same God's demand upon his creatures, 'You shall be holy as I am holy'. As the implications of this demand are sketched out in such central passages as the ten commandments and Jesus' Sermon on the Mount, it is indeed apparent that, while they certainly furnish very practical guides for the living of life in the world, offering standards and principles which can be pursued and approximated to in part, the overall vision of human holiness presented is one which it proves impossible in practice for anyone to achieve. It is, that is to say, a vision of a humanity which constantly *transcends* our lived actuality.

How are we to think of this? Precisely in eschatological terms, otherwise we shall quickly run into ethical (shortly followed by spiritual) languor. What we are offered in such passages is a model for imagining the shape of the new humanity which God will call into being when he brings history to its *telos*. There has only ever been one perfect parable of that new humanity within history: Jesus who, the New Testament writers tell us, fulfilled the law and kept the covenant. In Jesus God took upon himself the conditions of our 'old' humanity and, through the out-pouring of his Holy Spirit and through a triumphant human struggle with the powers of sin and death, fashioned for us out of it an eschatological sign, a flesh and blood pointer to and anticipation of the new humanity in the midst and under the form of the old; but in doing so he revealed just as surely that this new humanity does not belong or fit within the world as we know it now. It crops up as a scandal, a stumbling block, a freak which causes offence and must be put to death. We cannot bear it in our midst. Those who take upon themselves the yoke of following after this Jesus, offering resistance to the as yet still all too active forces of sin and death in the world, will discover this for themselves and at their own cost.

For us, and for now, this vision of a holy humanity, a

humanity characterized from first to last by the influence
of God's Holy Spirit rather than the principle of the 'flesh',
remains a vision of transcendence which stands in judgement over against our sinful and weak actuality. This much
Kant got right. But where do we go from here? Why is
such a vision offered to us at all? Why is it held out before
us if we find it impossible to grasp and to put into practice?
This is a question with which Kant struggled at length. Was
he not correct to construe it as an ideal towards which we
must strive in every situation? Yes and, as we shall see, an
understanding of the eschatological nature of this 'ideal'
both reinforces the need for such striving and (crucially)
furnishes the resources for its fruitful accomplishment. But
if the vision is no more than an ideal, then our repeated
failure to attain to it (for the fruitfulness of our striving is
and can only ever be a partial approximation to it),
especially when harnessed to a probative model of eschatology, leads naturally and inevitably to the evocation of
fear and self-concern as motivating forces underlying our
efforts. If, though, we suppose that in some identifiable
sense the only true motive for the pursuit of holiness, and
the force which finally transfigures patterns of behaviour,
relationships and institutions in this world, is not fear but
love, the sort of holy love which reflects God's own
character in the world, then the inherent flaw in Kant's
account becomes manifest. For, as a Scottish thinker was
to observe exactly sixty years after Kant committed his
thoughts to paper, we 'cannot be frightened into love'.[27]

If the biblical vision of human holiness is actually to
function as the spring of an *actual* holiness (however partial
and imperfect) in this life, therefore, if it is to cease to
hang over us like Damocles' sword, dripping with what
Steiner calls 'the blackmail of transcendence',[28] then it
must be understood eschatologically and seen not only as
an ideal but *also as a promise*. 'You shall be holy as I am

192

holy' is both; absolute demand and ultimate succour as one theologian has it.[29] It articulates not the condition *for* salvation but the ultimate condition *of* the saved. The God who calls us to holiness promises that, in due course, we shall indeed be clothed with it, and through his own efforts rather than ours. In the meanwhile, though, that promise, filled out in our imagination through reflection on the figure of Jesus in the gospels and the stories which he tells, and extrapolation to our own circumstances from the otherwise abstract ethical formulae of both testaments, remains fixed in our sights. By reshaping our self-understanding, our vision of what the future holds for us, and the shape of our basic desires, it lifts the tremendous burden of responsibility from our shoulders and liberates us to serve God, not now out of fear in a vain effort to save ourselves, but out of love, because we want to do so and because the good is something worth doing in itself.

ESCHATOLOGY AND THE LIBERATION OF THE OPPRESSED

Despite the ways in which it has sometimes been understood and used, eschatological orientation is neither a convenient excuse for the powerful to maintain the status quo nor a tool for the psychological manipulation of the morally lax. Eschatology is above all a source of hope and liberation, and is addressed, therefore, to those who, in one way or another, find themselves in the grip of hopelessness, slavery or oppression. The more other-worldly the focus, it seems, the more this-worldly its relevance. The more we are able to trust in God finally to transform the situation, the more we are lifted out of the mire of despair and set free to launch small-scale initiatives of resistance. It is no accident, therefore, that much of the explicitly eschatological literature in the Bible was written during periods of exile and persecution. It is directly political in nature, designed to shape the actions of the oppressed by capturing their imaginations and offering a transforming vision of God's promised future. Again, therefore, we see that the adjective 'eschatological' does not refer just to things which lie as yet in the remote future, but equally to the significance and impact of those same things for the present moment.

Sometimes this is done by imaginative accounts of what lies beyond history. In other examples we find visions of a much more this-worldly variety in which the present order of sin, death and oppression has already been overthrown and replaced within history by the forces of life and love. The eschatological image in Revelation 20 of a future millennial rule of the 'saints' of God,[30] for example, pictures those who, in the writer's present, were suffering terrible persecution for their attempt to follow Christ finally vindicated and rewarded for their faithfulness. Those who are martyred for Christ's sake, the story tells its hearers, and not those who currently hold power, will be the final victors in the struggle between light and darkness, good and evil; and the site of their vindication will be (at least as good as) the site of their humiliation and sacrifice. Such this-worldly portrayals do not have to be taken literally as predictive of the penultimate future of history in order to perform their liberating function.[31] Yet by presenting an account of the other-worldly in terms of the conditions of *this* world, such texts, as well as helping us to imagine the final victory in quite concrete terms, also remind us of its this-worldly and contemporary relevance, and encourage us in our imagining of and subsequent striving to realize anticipations of it in our own lives and those of our communities. To refer back to our typology in Chapter 4, imagination of a purely 'fantastic' sort would make the this-worldly dimensions of eschatological hope more difficult to appreciate.

Some further examples from Scripture will serve to reinforce our point in this section. First, chapters 40 to 55 of *Isaiah*, written from the estrangement of exile in Babylon at a time when the nation of Judah was effectively a nation no more; removed from the now ruined sanctuary of Zion around which her faith was focused, frogmarched in fetters some 700 miles east across the desert plains, broken on the wheel of events which were also the instrument of God's judgement. The land of promise, the land flowing with milk and honey, was now preserved and cherished only in her corporate memory, the theme of so many folk songs and tales designed to preserve a sense of national identity. The familiar words of the psalmist from this same era capture in a sentence or two what the hearts of the people must have felt: 'By the rivers of Babylon we sat and we wept when we remembered Zion. . . . How can we sing the songs of Yahweh in a strange land?' (Ps. 137:1–4).

Yet, curiously juxtaposed with such understandable lament, we find the green and vigorous shoots of new hope bursting through the arid and seemingly inhospitable soil of exile.

> 'Comfort my people, says your God. . . . In the wilderness prepare the way of Yahweh, make straight in the desert a highway for our God. . . . For a long time I have held my peace, I have kept still and restrained myself; now I will cry out like a woman in labour, I will gasp and pant. . . . Now thus says Yahweh, he who created you, O Jacob, he who formed you, O Israel: Do not fear, for I have redeemed you; I have called you by name, you are mine. . . . Do not remember the former things, or consider the things of old. I am about to do a new thing.'

And so it continues. As shrewd estimates of political reality go this can hardly number high on anyone's list. Yet *Isaiah* weaves a hopeful vision which contradicts the apparent realities of his people's circumstance, promising what seems beyond the bounds of current possibility, convinced that the redemptive capacities of the God who created all things cannot be circumscribed or measured by expectations rooted in the actual. In his imagination the prophet sees beyond the given to an unexpected and surprising future, a future in which his fellow Jews are able to find hope even in the midst of despair, renewed purpose in the face of servitude and an identity as the people of God which exile had threatened to obliterate. Holding firm to such a vision, the people will find that the present suffering loses its ultimacy and hence its capacity to crush the spirit.

Something similar may be observed in the book of *Revelation* to which we have already referred. Now, of course, it is the Christian church rather than the Jewish nation which finds itself in a form of exile in a world dominated by the forces of Roman empire. Writing to those for whom resistance to this regime and faithfulness to Christ may mean persecution, arrest and even death, John unfolds in his book what one of us has classified elsewhere as a 'prophetic apocalypse' which discloses through its imaginative form a transcendent perspective on this world and the events of contemporary history, setting them in the wider and fuller context of God's ultimate purposes for the coming of his kingdom. Thus:

> John (and thereby his readers with him) is taken up into heaven in order to see the world from the heavenly perspective. He is given a glimpse behind the scenes of history so that he can see what is really going on in the events of his time and place. He is also transported in vision into the final future of the world, so that he can see the present from the perspective of what its final outcome must be, in God's ultimate purpose for human history. The effect of

John's visions, one might say, is to expand his readers' world, both spatially (into heaven) and temporally (into the eschatological future), or, to put it another way, to open their world to divine transcendence. The bounds which Roman power and ideology set to the readers' world are broken open and that world is seen as open to the greater purpose of its transcendent Creator and Lord. It is not that the here-and-now are left behind in an escape into heaven or the eschatological future, but that the here-and-now look quite different when they are opened to transcendence.

The world seen from this transcendent perspective . . . is a kind of new symbolic world into which John's readers are taken as his artistry creates it for them. But really it is not another world. It is John's readers' concrete, day-to-day world seen in heavenly and eschatological perspective. As such its function . . . is to counter the Roman imperial view of the world, which was the dominant ideological perception of their situation which John's readers naturally tended to share.[32]

What we have here, then, is an imaginative vision in which the dominant way of seeing things (both present and future) is fundamentally challenged and an alternative picture painted of the potentialities and possibilities inherent in God's future. Rome is not the ultimate authority, and will not have the final victory. God is not absent, and his kingdom is coming. Whatever experience may suggest, and whatever the voices of power may insist, these are the realities of the readers' situation. The challenge to the Christian church in the midst of the all too real discomfort and danger of actuality is, as always, to live in the light of this alternative vision rather than submitting to the dominant ideology, even when the latter is backed up with military and political force. *Revelation*, like deutero-Isaiah, offers God's people a subversive vision, furnishing the resources to wage what theologian Amos Wilder calls a campaign of 'guerilla theatre', a battle for people's hearts and wills, and rooted firmly in a bid to capture their imaginations.[33]

REGENERATION AND RENEWAL

The conditions for the possibility of progress in this world are furnished by the reflexive impact of hope for God's transcendent future upon the here-and-now, an impact characterized not by fear and frenzied efforts to improve our chances, but by the liberation of discovering what it is that God wants to do for and with us. This discovery sets us free even now to be active in pursuit of correspondence to our eschatological destiny, confident in the knowledge that we shall not be forced to rely on our own resources in doing so, and set free from the otherwise crushing burden of responsibility for the ultimate outcomes. In our daily struggle with the patterns and forces of death, the Holy Spirit of life both sets us free from the bonds of the past and empowers us to move forward in hope, breathing new life into our shrivelled capacities and opening them up to receive a flow of power from God's promised future. Instead of being constrained by the prolongation of what has been and what is, we act in ways which are genuinely open to surprise, taking seriously the possibility of the advent of new and unpredictable manifestations of what will finally be, in the midst of the here-and-now. We live, in other words, in a present which is shaped by the future rather than the past, in the power of what we might call the future-made-present.[34] As Christians, then, we are not limited to a hope which simply imagines something which is, as yet, notable by its absence. In and through our imagining of it, and in and through the presence and agency in our midst of the Spirit who raised Jesus

198

from death, we actually experience what we hope for, albeit only in part and under the form of the things of this world. But in this way we are empowered to live history differently. In our experiences of this same Spirit 'God himself is present in us', and 'we are possessed by a hope which sees unlimited potentialities ahead, because it looks to God's future. The heart expands. The goals of hope in our own lives, and what we ourselves expect of life, fuse with God's promises for a new creation of all things.'[35]

A central biblical metaphor for this renewing of the present under the influence of the Spirit whose proper domain is the future is that of rebirth or regeneration. 'No one can see the kingdom of God,' Jesus tells Nicodemus, 'without being born from above. . . . What is born of the flesh is flesh, and what is born of the Spirit is spirit.'[36] The shock value of the metaphor did not slip past Nicodemus unnoticed. 'Can one enter a second time into the mother's womb and be born?' Clearly not. But the image is far from arbitrary. We have already suggested that the circumstances of Jesus' own birth as described in the gospels of Matthew and Luke offer a profound sign of this very same eschatological ambiguity. Life is brought forth where no potential for life naturally exists, and the agent is the same Holy Spirit. 'How can this be since I know not a man?' asks Mary. 'What do you mean "born from above"?' Nicodemus inquires. They are both good questions. Whether or not either Jesus himself or the author of the fourth gospel intended to trace the oblique but instructive connection between these passages, it is worth our while doing so.

Quite apart from this obvious suggestive source for Jesus' metaphor, it has plenty of independent imaginative force as a way of referring to what happens when the Spirit of Life comes. The limits of nature as we know and experience it (i.e. what is 'natural' or 'comes naturally' to us, what Jesus alludes to as 'the flesh') are broken open and,

in more or less radical and striking ways, the conditions
are created, within our individual lives and within history
more widely, for initiatives and events which are wholly
'new' with respect to what is otherwise and ordinarily possible and predictable. What is born of the flesh is flesh.
But what is born here, while it is in history's midst, is
decisively of the Spirit even though it encompasses the
material dimensions of our existence. (In the Bible the
realm of the Spirit is neither limited to nor coterminous
with the realm of the 'spiritual' in the sense of the extra-
material dimensions of our existence. There are plenty of
'spiritual' phenomena which cannot be ascribed to the
Spirit's activity, and discernment of these is itself an
important gift of the Holy Spirit.[37]) Thus, whether we are
thinking of those 'miracles' of healing and other remarkable physical phenomena which, in Jesus'own ministry or
in the subsequent experience of the church, finally must
be attributed to God's surprising and direct activity in
the world, or the equally miraculous transformation of
characters and transfiguration of communities through
faith and obedience, we are finally dealing with the same
thing: signs and anticipations of the eschatological
kingdom of God, the new creation and the new humanity
which God has promised. The forces of evil and death in
us and in our midst are being crucified, and the forces of
goodness and life in all its fullness born ('not of blood or
of the will of the flesh or of the will of man, but of God'[38])
within us.

The gradual renewal of this world to begin to fit the
pattern offered by another is thus aptly figured as birth,
the sudden appearance of scattered new initiatives of
'life', the antecedents for which cannot wholly be plotted
and traced at the level of natural causality. They are born,
as Jesus indicates, 'from the Spirit', 'from above', or, we
might venture to suggest, from God's promised future.

LIVING EXPECTANTLY

This does not mean, of course, that they are always achieved without our active involvement and effort. This, perhaps, is one drawback of the birth metaphor. Birth, after all, is something which happens to us quite apart from any willing or acting on our part. If we forget that birth is merely a beginning which throws us at once into a life of growth, development and struggle, then we shall be in danger of slipping into an eschatological 'wait and see', surrendering once again to the spirit of fear and limited possibilities who stalks this world. The fact that we cannot bring something about or render it possible in and of ourselves does not mean that its possibility will be established while we stand by and watch. This may sometimes have to be true, of course; but more often than not we may confidently expect that, while the Holy Spirit will do for us that which we cannot do for ourselves, he will nonetheless do it in and through us in ways which involve our full and free participation. It is in this very same willing and doing, in initiatives of 'inspired freedom', that progress becomes possible and the transformation of lives and communities takes place, at least in significant part.

Such willing and doing usually begins with the realization of our own human incapacity and the despair to which it leads. Having reached the end of their personal tether and heading for a breakdown of one sort or another, many have discovered for the first time the resources of God's Spirit in renewal. As one recent writer on this renewing activity puts it graphically: 'Sometimes God has to pull all the carpets out from under our feet, because it is only when we are flat on our backs, with our self-sufficiency shattered, that we will at last begin to look upwards to him.'[39] When we do so, though, we must expect the conse-

201

quences to be anything but comfortable. The logic of petition or intercession is a self-involving logic. We cannot pray, as Jesus teaches us to, 'Thy kingdom come, thy will be done on earth as it is in heaven' and plan then to sit back, having done our bit. To pray these words is to commit ourselves to an eschatological activism in which, through the power of the Spirit, we become part of the coming of God's kingdom, and spheres of the realization of his eternal will within history, no matter what the consequences of this may be for ourselves. For, as we have already noted, there is little biblical reason to suppose that participation in the renewing of this world by God's Spirit will lead to popularity, success or a quiet life. On the contrary, the degree to which the Spirit of Life is present and active seems to be the degree to which the forces of darkness and death home in for the kill, and are often allowed a temporary victory. The Spirit who raised Jesus from death is yet still the Spirit of the cross, and the road to renewal does not circumvent crucifixion but goes through it.[40] The things of this world need to be broken down in one way or another before they can be raised up anew. Furthermore, as the cross itself teaches us, the forces of death must sometimes be permitted a victory in order that their own redemption may be orchestrated.

Faithfulness to God's eschatological kingdom, participating in the Spirit's renewing work, may thus involve us directly in the associated suffering and humiliation of this process. Glib and triumphalistic appeals for God's 'power' in some theologies and spiritualities of 'renewal' would benefit from a reconsideration of this indisputable biblical fact: the one whose life and ministry was most clearly marked by that same power was driven at the last to a lonely and dark death on a cross. Nowhere in the New Testament is there any indication that those who follow in his footsteps should expect anything other or better for

202

themselves. The power of the Spirit which transforms lives and communities is fundamentally the power of life, and this takes shape humanly in history as the power of holy love, a love which seeks the good of the other even at the cost of its own denial or even death.

Such fearless self-giving is more likely to occur, though, where there is a superabundant hope of life upon which to draw.[41] Most readers of this book live in a society where the fear of death and loss holds the majority subconsciously in its grip, and where ideologies of self-advancement and the artificially stimulated appetite for 'more of everything good now' dominates our view of the world, our practical priorities, and our understanding of life's ultimate meaning and goal. The desire for 'more of everything good' is not necessarily perverse in itself. It might be seen as a legitimate recognition of that goodness of this world in its own right about which we spoke earlier, although it can develop into an unhealthy addiction incapable of satisfaction, a development which some (within the nexus of morally complex forces which is 'the market') have a vested interest in inculcating and then exploiting. Somewhere along the way we have become unquestioning consumers, and have lost sight of the genuine satisfaction that comes from limiting our consumption and sharing what we have with others, an arrangement from which both givers and recipients benefit and are blessed in a range of different and unexpected ways.

Where the desire for 'more now' is clearly perverse is in its assumption that particular individuals should either need or be able to amass more for the benefit of them-selves or their families, relatively regardless of the knock-on cost to others. Here the ideology of personal freedom to choose blurs together with selfish indifference to the common good, and so funds the spiral of debt and death. For the truth is, of course, that in practice in this life

203

resources are finite. If, therefore, one person gets more, then another somewhere will be getting less. Depending on how much there actually is overall, this may mean that some (perhaps many) will have less than they need in order to enjoy even a basic decent and humane standard of life, while others bloat themselves on excess, and hoard still more away for subsequent consumption. It does not take a rocket scientist to work this out, even though some economists and politicians seem unable or unwilling to accommodate its truth.

We are only too well aware of the ways in which, in actual fact, this disparity manifests itself in our world. The inequitable distribution of wealth, resources and oppor-tunities between rich and poor groups in the societies of the 'developed' nations, and between the 'developed' and the 'developing' nations, is no news to anyone, and appears to be getting worse rather than better. There are plenty of other, quite different, examples of injustice to be had from a brief trawl of stories from any daily newspaper. Whether it is power, money, opportunity, education, land, oil, food, clothing and shelter, healthcare or whatever; realizing that there is only so much to go around, the basic instinct of fallen humanity appears to be to grab as much of the best of it as we can get while it is still available, no matter who we may have to tread on in the rush. This, we suppose in some sense to be our 'right' so long as we can do it without breaching any legal barrier.

Ironically, it seems to be the case that the more we have the more fervently we submit to this impulse (those who have little are often the most generous in sharing it) and the more we think we need and are prepared to grab for ourselves. Of course those who have do regularly make what they have available to those who do not have and want it; but usually as a transaction from which the 'haves' themselves will eventually profit rather than as an act of justice, and at rates of interest which enslave and destroy. Such fundamental and institutionalized selfishness and injustice leads inevitably to conflict and violence. Those who do not have see even what little they have being torn gradually but surely from their weakening grasp, while those who have most cannot even begin to contemplate having less, and are determined to hold on to it at any cost. At present in our world some 450 million people have too little to feed themselves and their families adequately. The poorest nations in our world are trapped in an ever descending spiral of debt to the richest. These are macroscopic examples of a pattern which is replicated in different ways at local levels throughout our lives. Sooner or later in such circumstances someone will resort to physical force as a means to protect their interests, and then the spiral of violence leading to destruction is unleashed.

Our point here is not to advocate alternative social, political and ethical strategies; not because the gospel has no contribution to make to these, but simply because our space is limited. Our immediate purpose is necessarily less ambitious; namely, to point to a vital link between what we have sketched above and the fear of death. The forces of death do not only lead to death but derive much of their energy from its thrall. Death robs us all, sooner or later, of everything that is good in this life (as well as releasing us from its pains) and, 'because we know we have to die, we cannot get enough of living'.[42] We struggle for more because we are afraid that this is all there is, and there is not enough of it ever to satisfy our own boundless appetites, let alone to go around. This lack leads duly to the frenzied struggle for power and influence. These in their turn generate fear and suspicion of our competitors in the struggle for life, and breed resentment and aggression on the part of those who are less successful in this struggle.

205

Injustice breeds violence and leads to death. But injustice is itself the offspring of death, and it can only finally be redeemed by the hope of life in all its fullness.

It is this hope alone, kindled by the presence of the Holy Spirit, the giver of life, and focused on the assured promise of resurrection and eternal life, which can deliver us from the conditions of fear and anxiety which produce injustice and violence. Greed for life is what love for life becomes when it is limited by the fear of death. But once this fear is removed, we are set free from the security blanket which our earthly possessions become, and then we can give away what we have for the common good (even our life itself) without fearing that we shall lose out in doing so. For to have these things without this hope is to be haunted by an appetite which can never be satisfied. To have the hope, and to experience the reality of its power already through God's presence with us in the Spirit, is already to know a satisfaction and contentment which, while it certainly does not underestimate the goodness of such mundane things but rejoices in them, knows nonetheless that they are but the palest hints of that fullness of life which is yet to come, a life in which there will be no lack, but more than enough for all.

'Seek God's kingdom first,' says Jesus, 'and all this shall be given to you as well.' Live your lives in accordance with the long-term horizon of God's promise, rather than seeking short-term returns and making unjust investments in order to secure them. Seek whatever is consistent with God's justice. Resist the forces of death wherever and whenever you can identify them, either in yourselves or in the world. Defeat them with the power of love and self-sacrifice which bubbles up from the Spirit's presence and is the hallmark of his activity. Through this activity of discernment and resistance the spiral of sin and death can be reversed and broken, and the renewing forces of life released into the world.[43] This sort of 'spiritual warfare' is vital, not in order to generate the conditions for the new creation, but in order to value life in this world for its own sake, even though, ironically, it is something lying beyond this world which sets us free to do so.

Where does this leave us? If we turn to the Bible for guidance then we find clear indications that the Christian life is to be one of living expectantly; living each day, that is to say, in anticipation of the promised end and fulfilment of all things. In Jesus' teaching the stress is upon the urgency of preparation and the suddenness of the end when it actually comes. 'Keep awake therefore, for you do not know on what day your Lord is coming. . . . You . . . must be ready, for the Son of Man is coming at an unexpected hour.'[44] The point is not to encourage the sort of fascination with signs and portents which has led people throughout history to offer precise (and thus far erroneous) predictions of the day and hour. Nor should Jesus' words be taken as warrant for withdrawing from this-worldly concerns in order to prepare ourselves 'spiritually' for some imminent divine dispensing with the physical trappings of history. On the contrary, as we have seen, the sort of preparations which Jesus has in mind are very much this-worldly; the presence of the new creation already under the form of the old is to be recognized not in mystical fervour or some purifying detachment from the world, but precisely in radical involvement in the world, purifying *it* through initiatives for divine justice, peace and the life to which these lead. The church is not *of* the world because it has its heart and its true citizenship set elsewhere, in God's promised future; yet it is called to be *in* the world and to value the world for its own sake by living history in the light of what lies beyond it. The note of urgency in Jesus' teaching reflects the fact that, no matter how much time may be left, the task is one which demands all our energy and activity. This is a responsibility, and not an optional extra. It is of the very essence of what it means to be Christian, a follower of the Christ of God.

At the time of writing this there is still much discussion in the media about how the approaching turn of the millennium should best be celebrated. In the light of all that we have said about the state we are in as a society and a race it might be asked whether celebration is an appropriate thing to be doing at all. Of course everyone likes a party, and celebrating does help to distract us for a short while from the spiralling forces which are dragging us down ever further into despair. Does anyone really doubt, though, that the colour and excitement of the occasion will be followed by a profound sense of deflation as the reality of life in the real world dawns upon us again? Shall we have any spiritual resources to face the morning after the night before? Or is a well-deserved hangover all we can reasonably expect? More than one non-Christian commentator has already noticed the seeming obscenity of expending so much effort and money in order to amuse ourselves on the anniversary of Christ's birth, when there are so many pressing priorities to be faced in our world. This is no mere killjoy attitude but a serious ethical reflection on the state we are in and the heart of the Christian gospel, and we should be grateful that those outside the Christian community are able to recognize and remind us of something which we might otherwise be in danger of forgetting. A secular state cannot necessarily be expected to transcend the temptation to try to create a 'lasting' monument (however tacky) to its own achievements and to whip up the 'feelgood factor' among its citizens in the process; but surely it behoves the Christian church to mark this point on the calendar in some other way?

The suggestion that the church should focus on the theme of 'repentance' as a fitting way of entering the next thousand years of its history is likely to be greeted by some as evidence that, even after two millennia, Christians still do not know how to have a good time or to enjoy life! But if repentance is properly thought of not only as an attitude of contrition for past failure, but as a fresh acknowledgement of our own inadequacy in the face of life's challenges, an invitation to the God who is the only source of life in all its fullness to come and transfigure our lives through his presence and activity, and thus as a conscious turning from the ways of death actively to embrace a new way of living, then the questions of where and how and by whom exactly 'life' is to be 'enjoyed' are blown wide open for fresh consideration rather than answered. It is only through such deliberate refocusing of our lives and priorities, aligning them with what God is doing and wills to do for and in us, that the possibility of progress, the overcoming of death by life, is to be had. To discover this and act upon it is to live in hope. The only alternative is the hopelessness engendered by more of the same.

What, then, might the church's role be at this particular juncture in history when secular sources of hope have withered and all but died? If we are true to the universal scope of God's redemptive purpose then we cannot be content with turning inwards and expending all our energy in identity-affirming but (so far as the world is concerned) arcane and irrelevant activities. Yet nor can we simply allow the world, or even its needs, to set our agenda, else we shall quickly surrender our identity as followers of the Christ, and condemn ourselves to a rather different but equally damning form of irrelevance. The perceived polarity between identity and relevance need not arise, though, if we are true to the eschatological dimension and direction of Christian faith and discipleship. For, if we live in hope, a hope shaped decisively by the imaginative resources of Scripture, invested in the God who raised

Jesus from death and who loves life, and open to the boundless possibilities of the Holy Spirit whose domain is the future, then we shall truly *be* the church in a way that the church has often not been. In other words, we shall be a place *in* the world which is not properly *of* the world, the people who live up to the hilt in this life but with their sights set firmly on a horizon lying beyond it, and who therefore model for society how this life may be lived in hope even when hope seems hopeless. In so doing we shall not, of course, save the world. Only God can do that. But we shall be faithful to our primary calling to bear witness, and to call the world back to a belief in the God with whom alone there is genuine hope for its future.

Epilogue

ᴼᴼᴼᴼᴼᴼᴼᴼ

Hope as the Child of the Future

French Catholic poet Charles Péguy wrote his long theological poem, *The Portal of the Mystery of Hope* (1911), in a
period of despair about both political developments and
his own life. That hope is figured in the poem as a little
girl is surely connected with the fact that at this time it
was only his children who gave meaning to his life. Whatever other reasons for despair, virtually everyone works for
their children. Small children are a natural symbol of hope
for the future even when there may be no other cause to
hope. 'Thus, without exception, all the world works for
the little girl hope.'[1]

While the small child may be a natural symbol of hope,
hope is far from natural. Writing in the face of a dark
future, Péguy thought hope an astonishing miracle, by
comparison with which the other two theological virtues,
faith and love (charity), seemed obvious and virtually to
be expected. Faith sees only what is, in time and eternity,
God and creation. Charity loves only what is, in time and
eternity, God and the neighbour. Hope, on the other hand,
sees and loves what will be in time and eternity.

> Hope sees what has not yet been and what will be,
> She loves what has not yet been and what will be.
> In the future of time and of eternity.[2]

So astonishing is it that people who see how things are
going today still hope for things to go better tomorrow

211

that it surprises even God.[3] 'I can't get over it,' Péguy engagingly has God say.[4] But the surprise is God's doing, the most remarkable of the fruits of his grace.

Perhaps the time for Péguy's image of hope as a little child has come. For too long the modern ideology of progress has pictured hope as grown-up, as the triumph of humanity come of age, taking its destiny into its own hands and creating the future for itself. More recently this vision has turned against hope, as supposedly mature humanity has come to seem more like a barbarous army, marching with aggressive determination to conquer the future, trampling everything in its path, progressive only in its mastery of ever more powerful and sophisticated means of destruction. Can the modern enterprise of hope be redeemed from despair? Perhaps only by Péguy's little girl hope, whom he pictures between her elder sisters, faith and charity, hanging on their arms, swinging along as children do. Tiny as she is, it looks as though she is being carried, lacking the energy to walk, pulled along the road by her sisters. In reality, it is she who moves the other two.[5] Young as she is, she lacks the temptations and the vices of maturity, its blindness to its own limitations, its hubris. She is trusting, as little children are, swinging along on the arms of others, but in reality she achieves far more than an observer would imagine. It is the little girl hope for whom the whole world works, claims Péguy.

Hope does not grow up. In an age of fading and lost hopes, this is, so to speak, the hope for hope. Hope must always be born anew: 'the little girl hope is she who forever begins.'[6]

Notes

ᴏᴏᴏᴏᴏᴏᴏᴏᴏ

PREFACE

1. R. Bauckham ed., *God Will Be All in All: The Eschatology of Jürgen Moltmann* (Edinburgh: T. & T. Clark, 1999). The book is a discussion especially of Moltmann's eschatology in his *The Coming of God*, tr. M. Kohl (London: SCM Press, 1996).

CHAPTER 1: The Decline of Secular Hope

1. G. Swift, *Waterland* (London: Heinemann, 1983) 291.
2. Quoted in H. Schwartz, *Century's End: A Cultural History of the Fin de Siècle from the 990s through the 1990s* (New York: Doubleday, 1990) 275.
3. M. Nordau, *Degeneration* (London, 1895) 2, quoted in C. Townshend, 'The Fin de Siècle', in A. Dancher ed., *Fin de Siècle: The Meaning of the Twentieth Century* (London: Tauris, 1995) 201.
4. Quoted in D. Thompson, *The End of Time: Faith and Fear in the Shadow of the Millennium* (London: Random House, 1997) 119.
5. Townshend, 'The Fin de Siècle', 202.
6. Townshend, 'The Fin de Siècle', 208–209.
7. Townshend, 'The Fin de Siècle', 207–208.
8. For this paragraph, see Thompson, *The End of Time*, chapter 5.
9. In the famous case of the year 1000, when popular eschatological expectation focused on an AD date, ordinary people were dependent on the scholars for calendrical data they would not otherwise have been aware of.
10. E.g. R. Williams, *Towards 2000* (London: Chatto & Windus/ Hogarth Press, 1983); R. M. Kidder ed., *An Agenda for the 21st Century* (Cambridge, Massachusetts: MIT Press, 1987); J. Kleist

and B. A. Butterfield ed., *Breakdowns: The Destiny of the Twentieth Century* (New York: Peter Lang, 1994); Dancher ed., *Fin de Siècle*, P. N. Stearns, *Millennium III, Century XXI* (Boulder, Colorado/ Oxford: Westview Press, 1998).

11. J. G. de Beus, *Shall We Make the Year 2000?: The Decisive Challenge to Western Civilization* (London: Sidgwick & Jackson, 1985).

12. S. Dunant and R. Porter ed., *The Age of Anxiety* (London: Virago, 2nd edition 1997) xv.

13. G. Watts, 'Can Science Reassure?', in Dunant and Porter ed., *The Age of Anxiety*, 187. It is typical that his account of science makes no reference to the commercial motives that direct most scientific research.

14. The phrase derives from Mircea Eliade.

15. It is worth noting the rarely recognized point that the myth of progress has here its own version of the 'scandal of particularity', so often held against Christianity in Enlightenment critiques of it. The myth of progress privileges people in proportion to their chronological place on the forward-moving path of progress, just as it privileges those who at any one time are in the vanguard of progress by contrast with the 'under-developed' world.

16. G. Steiner, *Errata: An Examined Life* (London: Weidenfeld & Nicolson, 1997) 103.

17. F. Dostoevsky, *The Karamazov Brothers* (trans. I. Avsey; Oxford: Oxford University Press, 1994) 297–308.

18. A useful introduction to his work is the anthology of topically arranged excerpts: R. J. Hollingdale ed., *A Nietzsche Reader* (Harmondsworth: Penguin, 1977).

19. F. Nietzsche, *The Gay Science*, translated by W. Kaufmann (New York: Random House, 1974) 273–274 (§341) (italics original).

20. W. Benjamin, *Illuminations* (ed. H. Arendt; tr. H. Zohn; New York: Schocken, 1969) 257–258; and cf. R. Alter, *Necessary Angels: Tradition and Modernity in Kafka, Benjamin and Scholem* (Cambridge, Massachusetts: Harvard University Press, 1991) 114–115.

21. J.-F. Lyotard, *The Postmodern Condition* (trans. G. Bennington and B. Massumi; Minneapolis: University of Minnesota Press, 1984) xxiv.

22. J.-F. Lyotard, *Postmodern Fables*, translated by G. Van Den Abbeele (Minneapolis: University of Minnesota Press, 1997) chapter 6.

23. Lyotard, *Postmodern Fables*, 100.

24. Though too complex to be labelled an anti-metanarrative, John Updike's remarkable novel, *Toward the End of Time* (Harmondsworth: Penguin, 1999), an evocation of mortality and futility in the early twenty-first century, puts quantum physics, scientific cosmology and evolution (stripped of its nineteenth-century assimilation to progress) in the place religious or progress-ivist humanist metanarratives would have occupied in earlier times. E.g.: 'The sun is a star. Christianity said, God is a man. Humanism said, Man is a god. Today the sages say, via such Jainist cosmogonies as string theory and the inflationary hypothesis, that everything is nothing. The cosmos is a free lunch, a quantum fluctuation' (p. 34).

CHAPTER 2: The Hope of an Ending

1. N. Williams, *Four Letters of Love* (London: Picador, 1998) 340.
2. J. Chesneaux, *Brave Modern World: The Prospects for Survival* (tr. D. Johnstone, K. Bowie and F. Garvie; London: Thames & Hudson, 1992) 17; H. Bertens, *The Idea of the Postmodern: A history* (London: Routledge, 1995) 227–229; D. Harvey, *The Condition of Postmodernity* (Oxford: Blackwell, 1990) 284–387.
3. H. Nowotny, 'From the future to the extended present', in G. Kirsch, P. Nijkampp and K. Zimmermann eds., *The Formulation of Time Preferences in a Multidisciplinary Perspective: The Consequences for Individual Behaviour and Collective Decision-Making* (Wissenschafts-zentrum Berlin Publications; Aldershot: Avebury, 1988) 29.
4. See the survey in J. Moltmann, *The Coming of God* (trans. M. Kohl; London: SCM Press, 1996) 218–226.
5. F. Fukuyama, *The End of History and the Last Man* (London: Penguin, 1992).
6. For a not unsympathetic critique, see C. Brown, 'The End of History?', in Dancher ed., *Fin de Siècle*, 1–19. Brown points out that Fukuyama commits the same mistake as the whole tradition of Enlightenment progressivism which he inherits: he universalizes the western perspective on the world.
7. Quoted in J. Moltmann, *The Coming of God*, 224.
8. Chesneaux, *Brave Modern World*, 26.
9. Cf. G. Mulgan in Dunant and Porter ed., *The Age of Anxiety*, 6: 'we gain control and lose it simultaneously.'

10. J.-F. Lyotard, *The Postmodern Condition*, xxiv.

11. The 2nd of January Group, *After Truth: A Post-modern Manifesto* (London: Inventions Press, 1986), quoted in R. Kearney, *The Wake of Imagination* (London: Routledge, 2nd edition, 1994) 360.

12. B. Hardy quoted in B. Wicker, *The Story-Shaped World* (London: Athlone Press, 1975) 47.

13. F. Kermode, *The Sense of an Ending* (London: Oxford University Press, 1967) 64.

14. This is Kermode's point in the words of M. L. Cook, *Christology as Narrative Quest* (Collegeville, Minnesota: Liturgical Press, 1997) 55.

15. Wicker, *The Story-Shaped World*, 135.

16. Kermode, *The Sense of an Ending*, 155.

17. Kermode, *The Sense of an Ending*, 179.

18. Quoted in P. T. Forsyth, *The Justification of God* (London: Duckworth, 1916) 223.

19. W. Pannenberg, 'Eschatology and the Experience of Meaning', in *Basic Questions in Theology*, vol. 3 (trans. R. A. Wilson; London: SCM Press, 1973) 192–210.

20. See R. Haughton, *Tales from Eternity* (London: Allen & Unwin, 1973) chapter 6.

21. For the importance of the category of story in Christian theology, see the first book in this series: S. W. Sykes, *The Story of Atonement* (London: Darton, Longman and Todd, 1997).

22. P. Kampits, 'Breakdowns: The Destiny of the Twentieth Century', in J. Kleist and B. A. Butterfield ed., *Breakdowns: The Destiny of the Twentieth Century* (New York: Peter Lang, 1994) 11.

CHAPTER 3: The Wager on Transcendence

1. Jonathan Sacks, *Faith in the Future* (London: Darton, Longman and Todd, 1995) 150.

2. Helen Gardner, *Religion and Literature* (London: Faber, 1971) 22.

3. The metaphor of life as tragedy will not be pushed too far since, as Iris Murdoch reminds us, the contrivance of the art form (like the essential detachment of the audience) is an essential part of the concept and the experience of tragedy. See Murdoch, *Metaphysics as a Guide to Morals* (London: Chatto and Windus, 1992) 92f.

4. William Shakespeare, *King Lear*, Act 1, scene 1.

5. 'ABANDON EVERY HOPE, ALL YOU WHO ENTER'. Dante Alighieri, *The Inferno*, Canto III.9. See Mark Musa (ed.) *The Portable Dante* (London: Penguin, 1995) 14.

6. Cf., for example, Kant's suggestion that in tragedy the sublime ('the proud energetic fear with which the rational being faces the contingent dreadfulness of the world') and the beautiful are fused in such a way as to offer 'a temporary, perhaps edifying, simulation of sanctity' even in characters whose history is one which in itself we should hardly find edifying. See Murdoch, *Metaphysics as a Guide to Morals*, 100.

7. William F. Lynch, *Images of Hope: Imagination as Healer of the Hopeless* (Dublin: Helicon, 1965) 21.

8. Shakespeare, *King Lear*, Act 5, scene 3.

9. See, e.g., Don Cupitt, *Radicals and the Future of the Church* (London: SCM Press, 1989) 15.

10. George Steiner, *Real Presences: Is there anything in what we say?* (London: Faber, 1989) 227.

11. Steiner, *Real Presences*, 226. See also 3–4.

12. The phrase 'a fiction of resolution' was coined in a different context by Deirdre David in *Fictions of Resolution in Three Victorian Novels* (New York: Columbia University Press, 1981), quoted in Edward Said, *Culture and Imperialism* (London: Vintage, 1994) 91.

13. Gardner, *Religion and Literature*, 89.

14. Herman Melville, *Moby Dick* (London: Penguin Popular Classics, 1994) 26.

15. Lynch, *Images of Hope*, 31. Original emphasis.

16. Lynch, *Images of Hope*, 44.

17. George Steiner, *After Babel* (2nd edn., Oxford: Oxford University Press, 1992) 145.

18. Steiner, *After Babel*, 168.

19. Steiner, *After Babel*, 167.

20. Steiner, *After Babel*, 228.

21. Lynch, *Images of Hope*, 35.

22. Moltmann, *Theology of Hope* (London: SCM Press, 1967) 21.

23. Bloch, *The Principle of Hope* (3 volumes, Oxford: Blackwells, 1986) 451.

24. Shakespeare, *King Lear*, Act 1, scene 1.

25. Kearney, *The Wake of Imagination*, 359.

26. Ziauddin Sardar, *Postmodernism and the Other: The New Imperialism of Western Culture* (London: Pluto Press, 1998) 62.
27. Kearney, *The Wake of Imagination*, 367–8.
28. Kearney, *The Wake of Imagination*, 361f.
29. From 'One God' on the 1997 album *blue is the colour* by The Beautiful South.
30. Samuel Beckett, *Waiting for Godot* (2nd edn, London: Faber, 1965) 53–4.
31. Kearney, *The Wake of Imagination*, 360.
32. Lynch, *Images of Hope*, 40.
33. Bloch, *The Principle of Hope*, 144.
34. Lynch, *Images of Hope*, 65.
35. 2 Corinthians 1:9, NRSV.
36. John 3:7.
37. See, for example, *The Coming of God* (London: SCM Press, 1996) 28.
38. Revelation 21:5, NRSV.
39. See the powerful reflections of Steiner, *Real Presences*, 231–2.

CHAPTER 4: Ambiguous Vision

1. Augustine, *City of God*, Book 21, ch. 4.
2. Historicism used the same method to construct history, assuming that what happened in the past must, in broad outlines at least, be fundamentally similar (analogous) to what we experience in the present. See further on this Karl Popper, *The Poverty of Historicism* (London: Routledge, 1957).
3. Rudolf Bultmann, *Jesus Christ and Mythology* (London: SCM Press, 1958) 23.
4. Jürgen Moltmann, *Theology of Hope* (London: SCM Press, 1967) 226.
5. Compare Tzvetan Todorov, *The Fantastic: A Structural Approach to a Literary Genre* (New York: Cornell University Press, 1975) and Rosemary Jackson, *Fantasy: the Literature of Subversion* (London: Methuen, 1981) for helpful treatments of the issues raised in this section.
6. Russ, 'The Subjunctivity of Science Fiction' in *Extrapolation*, 15:1, 52. Cited in Jackson, *Fantasy*, 22.

7. W. Irwin, *The Game of the Impossible: A Rhetoric of Fantasy* (Illinois, 1976) p.x. Cited in Jackson, *Fantasy*, 14.

8. R. Caillois, *Au Coeur du Fantastique*, cited in Todorov, *The Fantastic*, 26.

9. Jackson, *Fantasy*, 48.

10. Freud, cited in Jackson, *Fantasy*, 8.

11. Jackson, *Fantasy*, 20.

12. See *The Fantastic*, chapter 3.

13. Jackson, *Fantasy*, 33.

14. Jackson, *Fantasy*, 20.

15. Todorov, *The Fantastic*, 25.

16. Jackson's term 'mode' seems preferable to 'genre' since, as Todorov's own analysis makes quite clear, it is perfectly possible for fantasy to be resolved into some other mode within a given text.

17. Charles Williams, *The Place of the Lion* (London: Victor Gollancz, 1931).

18. Williams, *The Place of the Lion*, 63.

19. The phrase is borrowed from J. Bellemin-Noel, 'Des Formes fantastiques aux themes fantasmatiques' in *Litterature*, 2 (May 1971), p.112. Cited in Jackson, *Fantasy*, 38.

20. Jackson, *Fantasy*, 38–9.

21. It is perhaps unsurprising that many commentators have either decided that verse 17 is rhetorical hyperbole, not to be taken seriously, or that its connection with what follows is a later attempt to give the passage an apocalyptic flavour.

CHAPTER 5: Images of Hope

1. H. de Lubac, *The Discovery of God* (tr. A. Dru; Edinburgh: T. & T. Clark, 1996) 193.

2. C. Zaleski, *The Life of the World to Come: Near-Death Experience and Christian Hope* (New York/Oxford: Oxford University Press, 1996) 47.

3. U. Simon, *The End is Not Yet* (London: Nisbet, 1964) 160.

4. A notable exception is Simon, *The End is Not Yet*, chapter 13.

5. H. Urs von Balthasar, *The Glory of the Lord*, vol. 3 (tr. A. Louth, J. Saward, M. Simon, R. Williams; Edinburgh: T. & T. Clark, 1986) 296. Von Balthasar is here writing of the role of the Antichrist in the work of the Russian philosopher-theologian Vladimir Soloviev.

6. From 'The Antichrist', in E. Muir, *Collected Poems* (London: Faber 1984) 226.

7. The authorship of 2 Thessalonians is disputed, but the point is of no importance to us here.

8. For this correspondence to reality, see R. Bauckham, *The Climax of Prophecy: Studies on the Book of Revelation* (Edinburgh: T. & T. Clark, 1993) chapters 10–11.

9. The only book that attempts to survey the whole history is B. McGinn, *Antichrist: Two Thousand Years of the Human Fascination with Evil* (San Francisco: HarperCollins, 1994); but see also W. Bousset, *The Antichrist Legend* (tr. A. H. Keane; London: Hutchinson, 1896); G. C. Jenks, *The Origin and Development of the Antichrist Myth* (BZNW 59; London/New York: de Gruyter, 1991); R. K. Emmerson, *Antichrist in the Middle Ages* (Manchester: Manchester University Press, 1981); R. Muir Wright, *Art and Antichrist in Mediaeval Europe* (Manchester: Manchester University Press, 1995); R. Bauckham, *Tudor Apocalypse* (Appleford: Sutton Courtenay Press, 1979); C. Hill, *Antichrist in Seventeenth Century England* (Oxford: London University Press, 1971).

10. Cf. M. Slouka, *War of the Worlds: Cyberspace and the High-Tech Assault on Reality* (New York: BasicBooks, 1995).

11. J. Moltmann, *Theology of Hope* (tr. J. W. Leitch; London: SCM Press, 1967) 17.

12. Quotation attributed to the World Council of Churches in E. Stackhouse, *The End of the World?: A New Look at an Old Belief* (New York/Mahwah: Paulist Press, 1997) vii.

13. For a fuller discussion of the place of the parousia in a narrative Christology, see R. Bauckham, 'The Future of Jesus Christ (Finlayson Memorial Lecture 1998)', *Scottish Bulletin of Evangelical Theology* 16 (1998) 97–110.

14. So J. D. G. Dunn, 'He Will Come Again', *Interpretation* 51 (1997) 42–56.

15. J. Harward ed., *John Donne: A Selection of his Poetry* (Harmondsworth: Penguin, 1950) 170.

16. From 'That Nature is a Heraclitean Fire and of the Comfort of the Resurrection.' in W. H. Gardner ed., *Poems and Prose of Gerard Manley Hopkins* (Harmondsworth: Penguin, 1953) 66.

17. E.g. P. Badham, *Christian beliefs about Life after Death* (London: Macmillan, 1976). We could add that nor is it based on the kind

of evidence for survival of death which 'near-death experiences' are understood by some to provide; cf. P. and L. Badham, *Immortality or Extinction?* (London: Macmillan, 1982).

18. There is broad agreement among commentators on this point; see, e.g., M. J. Harris, *Raised Immortal: Resurrection and Immortality in the New Testament* (London: Marshall, Morgan & Scott, 1983) 119–121; B. Witherington, *Conflict and Community in Corinth: A Socio-Rhetorical Commentary on 1 and 2 Corinthians* (Grand Rapids: Eerdmans/Carlisle: Paternoster, 1995) 308–309.

19. K. Barth, *Church Dogmatics* III/2 (Edinburgh: T. & T. Clark, 1960) 624; W. Pannenberg, *The Apostles' Creed in the Light of Today's Questions* (tr. M. Kohl; London: SCM Press, 1972) 174–175; idem, *Systematic Theology*, vol. 3 (tr. G. W. Bromiley; Grand Rapids: Eerdmans/Edinburgh: T. & T. Clark, 1998) 606–607; J. Moltmann, *The Coming of God* (tr. M. Kohl; London: SCM Press, 1996) 71, 84–85.

20. E. Brunner, *Eternal Hope* (tr. H. Knight; London: Lutterworth, 1954) 203.

21. *Hymns on Paradise* 9.1, in St Ephrem, *Hymns on Paradise* (tr. S. Brock; New York: St Vladimir's Seminary Press, 1990) 136.

22. Moltmann, *The Coming of God*, 202.

23. *Divine Institutes* 7.24, tr. in B. McGinn ed., *Apocalyptic Spirituality: Treatises and Letters of Lactantius, Adso of Montier-en-Der, Joachim of Fiore, the Franciscan Spirituals, Savonarola* (London: SPCK, 1979) 73.

24. For the exegetical debate and the various classic interpretative positions, see (among many) R. G. Clouse, *The Meaning of the Millennium: Four Views* (Downers Grove: InterVarsity Press, 1977); J. W. Mealy, *After the Thousand Years: Resurrection and Judgment in Revelation 20* (JSNTSS 70; Sheffield: JSOT Press, 1992) chapters 2–3; S. J. Grentz, *The Millennial Maze* (Downers Grove: InterVarsity Press, 1992).

25. For a brief conspectus of millenarianism in the Christian tradition, see R. Bauckham, 'Millenarianism', in P. B. Clarke and A. Linzey ed., *Dictionary of Ethics, Theology and Society* (London/New York: Routledge, 1996) 565–569.

26. Here we reproduce the argument in R. Bauckham, *The Theology of the Book of Revelation* (Cambridge: Cambridge University Press, 1993) 106–108. On the theological meaning of the millennium in Revelation 20, see now also M. Gilbertson, *The Meaning of the*

Millennium (Grove Biblical Series 5; Cambridge: Grove Books, 1997).

27. For a thousand years as representing an extremely long period see Ps. 90:4.

28. On this paragraph, see further R. Bauckham, 'Approaching the Millennium', forthcoming in *Anvil* (1999).

29. On this see Moltmann's insightful reading of millenarian history, in which the triumphalism of realized millenarianism must always oppose and suppress eschatological millenarianism: J. Moltmann, *The Coming of God*, Part III; and see the discussion by R. Bauckham, 'The Millennium': chapter IV/1 in R. Bauckham ed., *God Will Be All in All: The Eschatology of Jürgen Moltmann* (Edinburgh: T. & T. Clark, 1999) 123–147.

30. 'Judgment', in J. N. Wall, Jr. ed., *George Herbert: The Country Parson, the Temple* (New York/Mahwah: Paulist Press, 1981) 314–315.

31. E.g. E. Hill, *Being Human: A Biblical Perspective* (London: G. Chapman, 1984) 269–270.

32. From Jorge Luis Borges, 'Adam Cast Forth', tr. A. Reid, in D. Curzon ed., *Modern Poems on the Bible: An Anthology* (Philadelphia/Jerusalem: Jewish Publication Society, 1994) 81.

33. Simon, *The End Is Not Yet*, 179.

34. Probably the most ambitious attempt to construct a garden replicating paradise is the Taj Mahal.

35. Medieval theologians distinguished the three states of humanity: before the fall: *posse non peccare* (able not to sin); after the fall: *non posse non peccare* (not able not to sin); and in the resurrection: *non posse peccare* (not able to sin).

36. R. Bauckham, 'Jesus and the Wild Animals (Mark 1:13): A Christological Image for an Ecological Age', in J. B. Green and M. Turner ed., *Jesus of Nazareth: Lord and Christ : Essays on the Historical Jesus and New Testament Christology* (I. H. Marshall FS; Grand Rapids: Eerdmans, 1994) 9.

37. E. Eisenberg, *The Ecology of Eden* (London: Picador, 1998) 84.

38. By Pär Andersson, 1985.

39. Translation by Helen Waddell, *Mediaeval Latin Lyrics* (Harmondsworth: Penguin, 1952) 177.

40. *The Tree of Life* 47, tr. E. Cousins, in E. Cousins ed., *Bonaventure: The Soul's Journey into God; The Tree of Life; The Life of St. Francis* (London: SPCK, 1978) 171–172.

41. See the reproductions in MacDannell and Lang, *Heaven*, 129, 131; or E. Morante ed., *L'opera completa dell' Angelico* (Milan: Rizzoli Editore, 1970) Plates 4–5.

42. C. S. Lewis, *Letters to Malcolm: Chiefly on Prayer* (London: Bles, 1964) 122.

43. *Serm.* 362.28.29, quoted in B. E. Daley, *The Hope of the Early Church: A Handbook of Patristic Eschatology* (Cambridge: Cambridge University Press, 1991) 146.

44. See Daley, *The Hope of the Early Church*, 88, on Gregory of Nyssa; and, following Gregory, G. W. H. Lampe, *God as Spirit* (Oxford: Clarendon, 1977) 175: 'Not only is there progress in perfection, but human perfection, unlike that of changeless deity, actually consists in progress. . . . True fulfilment, the completion of man's creation, consists in endless progress, an unceasing ascent in which the continual satisfaction of desire begets further desire for that which, since man is but a creature, remains eternally beyond his grasp.'

45. See especially C. McDannell and B. Lang, *Heaven: A History* (New Haven/London: Yale University Press, 1988) chapter 9.

46. A. N. Wilson (in D. Cohn-Sherbok and C. Lewis ed., *Beyond Death* [Basingstoke/London: Macmillan, 1995] 197) is right to observe that 'the most deliriously happy moments in life have come when we have forgotten ourselves', but his further assertion that to survive death 'would be horrible . . . a fate far worse than death itself' betrays a lack of imagination.

47. B. D. Chilton, *Pure Kingdom: Jesus' Vision of God* (Grand Rapids: Eerdmans/London: SPCK, 1996) 16.

48. H. Desroches, *The Sociology of Hope* (tr. C. Martin-Sperry; London: Routledge, 1979) 113 (italics in the original have been removed).

49. What follows here draws partly on R. Bauckham, 'Kingdom and Church according to Jesus and Paul', *Horizons in Biblical Theology* 18 (1996) 1–26, where some aspects are treated in more detail.

50. Mark 4:26–32; Matt. 13:31–33.

51. In the single exception, Matt. 5:35, he is alluding to Ps. 48:2.

52. J. D. Crossan, *The Historical Jesus: The Life of a Mediterranean Jewish Peasant* (Edinburgh: T. & T. Clark, 1991) 266.

53. Tr. H. Waddell, in F. Corrigan ed., *Between Two Eternities: A Helen Waddell Anthology* (London: SPCK, 1993) 185.

54. *De Civitate Dei* 22.30, tr. H. Bettenson in Augustine, *Concerning the*

City of God against the Pagans (Harmondsworth: Penguin, 1972) 1088.

55. This was the view of, for example, Joseph Hall, quoted in McDannell and Lang, *Heaven*, 173.

56. McDannell and Lang, *Heaven*, 357.

CHAPTER 6: Breaking the Spiral

1. Matt Redman, 'Now to live the life' from the album *Intimacy*, Survivor Records, 1998.

2. Peter Atkins, *Creation Revisited* (Harmondsworth: Penguin, 1994) 23.

3. See above Chapter 3.

4. See John Baillie, *And the Life Everlasting* (London: Oxford University Press, 1934) chapters 1 and 2.

5. See Jürgen Moltmann, *God for a Secular Society: The Public Relevance of Theology* (London: SCM Press, 1999) 88–91.

6. Horace Shipp, *The Italian Masters, a Survey and Guide*, 79 (cited in Baillie, *And the Life Everlasting*, 12).

7. See, e.g., *Phaedo* 64 in Loeb Classical Library Vol. 36, 229, 223.

8. 2 Cor. 5:6,8 (NRSV).

9. *The Methodist Hymn Book* (London, 1933) No. 658.

10. 'How Apocalypticism Constrains God's Future: Toward an Evolutionary Eschatology' in *Dialog*, Vol. 37.4 (Fall 1998) 271.

11. Nessan, 272.

12. This distinction is helpfully made, e.g., by Baillie, *And the Life Everlasting*, 28.

13. George Steiner, *In Bluebeard's Castle or Some Notes Towards a Redefinition of Culture* (London: Faber, 1971) 56.

14. Charles Mackay, *Memoirs of Extraordinary Popular Delusions and the Madness of Crowds* (London, 1852) 257, cited in Damian Thompson, *The End of Time: Faith and Fear in the Shadow of the Millennium* (London: Random House, 1997) 36.

15. Thompson, *The End of Time*, 36.

16. Marilyn Ferguson, *The Aquarian Conspiracy: Personal and Social Transformation in the 1980s* (London: Paladin, 1982) 24–5. Italics original.

17. See above, Chapter 2.

18. Gen. 1:10,12, 18, 21, etc.

19. Moltmann, *The Coming of God*, 50.
20. Steiner, *In Bluebeard's Castle*, 48.
21. See Richard Bauckham, 'Universalism: a Historical Survey' in *Themelios* 4:2 (1979).
22. Immanuel Kant, *Religion within the Boundaries of Mere Reason and Other Writings* (Cambridge: Cambridge University Press, 1998) 86.
23. Kant, *Religion within the Boundaries*, 136.
24. See Kant, *Religion within the Boundaries*, 204–5. The point is developed more fully in Kant's second Critique.
25. See, for example, the following statements: 'Moreover, it never seems advisable to be encouraged to such a state of confidence but much more beneficial (for morality) to "work out one's salvation with *fear* and *trembling*" (a hard saying which, if misunderstood, can drive one to the darkest enthusiasm)' (85). 'The aim of those who have a clergyman summoned to them at the end of life is normally to find in him a comforter . . . At such a time, however, conscience ought rather to be *stirred up* and *sharpened* in order that whatever good yet to be done, or whatever consequences of past evil still left to be undone (repaired for), will not be neglected. . . . But to administer opium to conscience instead, as it were, is to be guilty of a crime against the human being himself and against those who survive him, and is totally contrary to the purpose for which such support given to conscience at life's end can be held necessary' (93, n.).
26. See Moltmann, *The Coming of God*, 55–6.
27. Thomas Erskine of Linlathen in a letter to Lord Rutherford, 8 November 1853.
28. See *In Bluebeard's Castle*, 40–41. What Kant presents as 'incentive' Steiner identifies as a crushing psychological burden which, he believes, lies behind the modern western effort to be rid not only of God but of the ultimate human bearers of his demand, the Jews. If this is indeed the ironic product of the divine demand for holiness, its only alternative is a proper recognition of that demand as equally a promise, and no less so in the Old Testament than in the New.
29. H. H. Farmer. See, e.g., *Revelation and Religion* (London: Nisbet, 1954) Chapter VII. See also Christopher Partridge, *H. H. Farmer's Theological Interpretation of Religion: Towards a Personalist Theology of Religions* (Lampeter: Edwin Mellen, 1998) 284f.

30. See Chapter 5 above.
31. For one recent treatment insisting that the image should be treated in this way see, however, Moltmann, *The Coming of God*, chapter III, esp. 192f.
32. R. Bauckham, *The Theology of the Book of Revelation* (Cambridge: Cambridge University Press, 1993) 7–8.
33. A. Wilder, *Theopoetic: Theology and the Religious Imagination* (Philadelphia: Fortress Press, 1976).
34. See Moltmann, *The Coming of God*, 22.
35. Moltmann, *The Spirit of Life* (London: SCM Press, 1992) 155.
36. John 3:3,6 (NRSV).
37. See, e.g., 1 Cor. 12:10.
38. See John 1:13.
39. Tom Smail in Tom Smail, Andrew Walker and Nigel Wright, *Charismatic Renewal: The Search for a Theology* (London: SPCK, 1995) 12.
40. See on this Smail, *Charismatic Renewal*, 58f.
41. What follows in the following paragraphs is largely indebted to a sermon preached in St Andrews Episcopal Church, St Andrews, in June 1997 by Professor Jürgen Moltmann on the theme 'There is enough for everyone'.
42. Moltmann, 'There is enough for everyone'.
43. See on this Walter Wink, *Engaging the Powers: Discernment and Resistance in a World of Domination* (Philadelphia: Fortress Press, 1992).
44. Matthew 24:42, 44 (NRSV).

EPILOGUE: Hope as the Child of the Future

1. C. Péguy, *The Portal of the Mystery of Hope* (tr. D. L. Schindler, Jr; Grand Rapids: Eerdmans, 1996) 22.
2. Péguy, *The Portal*, 11–12.
3. Péguy, *The Portal*, 6.
4. Péguy, *The Portal*, 7.
5. Péguy, *The Portal*, 12.
6. Péguy, *The Portal*, 23.

INDEX OF PERSONAL NAMES

Donne, J. 122
Dostoevsky, F. 16, 214
Dunant, S. 214, 215
Dunn, J. D. G. 220

Ecclesiastes 77, 78
Eisenberg, E. 151, 222
Eliade, M. 214
Emmerson, R. K. 220
Ephrem the Syrian 127, 221
Erskine, T. 225
Ezekiel 78

Farmer, H. H. 225
Ferguson, M. 224
Flaubert, G. 33
Forsyth, P. T. 216
Frederick II 114
Freud, S. 219
Fukuyama, F. 28, 215

Gardner, H. 50, 216, 217
Gardner, W. H. 220
Gilbertson, M. 221
Green, J. B. 222
Grentz, S. J. 221
Grimm Brothers 91

Hall, J. 224
Hardy, B. 31, 216
Harris, M. J. 221
Harrison, F. 5
Harvey, D. 215
Harward, J. 220
Haughton, R. 216
Hegel, G. W. F. 28
Herbert, G. 139

Hill, C. 220
Hill, E. 222
Hitler, A. 23
Hollingdale, R. J. 214
Hopkins, G. M. 122
Hussein, S. 114

Irenaeus of Lyons 136
Irwin, W. 219
Isaiah 78, 79

Jackson, R. 91, 96, 218, 219
Jenks, G. C. 220
Jeremiah 78
Jesus Christ *see Subject Index*
John, author of Revelation 69, 196, 197
John the Baptist 102
John XXII, Pope 114

Kampits, P. 216
Kant, I. 189, 190, 192, 217, 225
Kearney, R. 59, 216, 217, 218
Kermode, F. 32, 33, 216
Kidder, R. M. 213
Kirsch, G. 215
Klee, P. 23
Kliest, J. 213, 216

Lactantius 133
Lang, B. 223
Lampe, G. W. H. 223
Lang, A. 91, 224
Lear, King 47, 48
Lewis, C. 223
Lewis, C. S. 156, 223
Linzey, A. 221

SUBJECT INDEX